LOVE
NOT GIVEN
LIGHTLY

LOVE
NOT GIVEN
LIGHTLY

PROFILES FROM THE EDGE OF SEX

PORN STARS, PERVERTS, FEMME DOMMES, RENT BOYS, AND OTHER PROFESSIONAL LOVERS

TINA HORN

ThreeL Media | Berkeley

Published by
ThreeL Media | Stone Bridge Press
P. O. Box 8208, Berkeley, CA 94707
www.threelmedia.com

© 2015 Tina Horn

Cover design and interior illustrations by kd diamond.

Book design and layout by Linda Ronan.

LIBRARY OF CONGRESS CATALOGING-IN-PUBLICATION DATA
Horn, Tina.
 Love not given lightly : profiles from the edge of sex / Tina Horn.
    pages cm
 ISBN 978-0-9905571-0-4 (paperback)
 ISBN: 978-0-9905571-1-1 (e-book)
1. Sex customs—United States—History—21st century. 2. Sex (Psychology) I. Title.
 HQ18.U5H67 2015
 392.6—dc23
                            2015007288

*For my sweet bear
and all the professional lovers*

"We must not allow the paths of desire to become overgrown."

—ANDRE BRETON

"Power is what distinguishes the psychic discourse of desire from the social rhetoric of sex. . . . What we on the margins have been most able to appropriate of this discourse is the power analysis that so much of the discourse of patriarchy is structured precisely to mystify. In many cases, its demystification is precisely what has allowed us to survive."

—SAMUEL R. DELANY

"It's a business doin' pleasure with ya!"
—DOLLY PARTON, in

The Best Little Whorehouse in Texas

CONTENTS

Who the hell is **Tina Horn?**

introduction

Who the hell is Tina Horn?

December 2014
by *Tina Horn*

I wrote the stories in *Love Not Given Lightly* to explain how and why I was transformed into Tina Horn.

or;

I wrote these stories because Tina Horn transformed into me.

or maybe;

Tina Horn wrote these stories, and you can send all complaints her way.

Actually, I'm not convinced that Tina Horn exists. I'm not entirely convinced it's Tina Horn who is writing these words. Maybe it's actually *me*.

But am I not Tina Horn?

If not, then who the hell *is* she, and why is she always hogging the bathroom?

Tina Horn was born in 2006 (fully-formed and perfectly legal), when, looking for a flexible gig to support my rock & roll lifestyle, I typed the word "dominatrix" into the Adult Gigs section of San Francisco Craigslist.

Or, was she *in* me, archetypically, all along? Is Tina Horn *the real me*? An amplification of my id, a creature of camp and confidence and creative impulse who animates my body? Did I have to become a sex worker in order to unleash her?

Robert Zimmerman once told Rolling Stone: "I didn't create Bob Dylan. Bob Dylan has always been here."

Obviously, I am Tina Horn, and I know what it's like to Do, or Perform, Tina Horn. She looks like me, she sounds like me, and she finds the same things erotic. She puts more effort into her appearance, than I do. She's more agreeable, less cerebral. But, am I only Tina Horn when you're paying for my time? Am I Tina Horn when I sleep? When I die, will Tina Horn die too?

Most importantly: wardrobe and attitude and ontological status aside, what is Tina Horn *good for*?

Well, Tina Horn has made me some good money, for starters. Since 2006, I have worked as a professional **BDSM** switch, both in houses and as an independent, providing direct service fetish and fantasy exploration to clients who paid me an hourly rate. In 2009, I started to perform in independent, queer, and kinky hardcore videos in the Bay Area. In 2010, I began directing my own pornography,

BDSM stands for: Bondage, Discipline, Domination, Submission, Sadism, and Masochism.

and co-founded *QueerPorn.Tv*, a membership site that won two Feminist Porn Awards, a Cinekink Award, and an AVN nomination during the time I was a producer there. Throughout this era, I created and distributed zines about sex work, later publishing essays online and in magazines. I taught workshops on spanking and dirty talk, and spoke on college panels. After moving to New York City, I worked in advocacy for people in the sex trades, especially with the Persist Health Project.

Here's an excerpt from one of those zines, circa 2008.

> *Marxist critic Walter Benjamin used prostitutes as examples of dialectical images, where the commodity and seller are the same and reveal the system of representation that produces them. He was on to something, but somehow I doubt Benjamin ever strapped on six-inch stilettos and hogtied men for money (although, of course, we can never be sure).*

I can't remember exactly what I thought was going to happen when I created Tina Horn, but I know I got what I came for. Sex work is glamour and danger and boredom and drama and shock. Sex work is adrenaline highs and clandestine secrets and surprise orgasms. Sex work is a blue velvet Crown Royal bag stuffed full of lacy thongs, *Bitches Brew* on an Ipod shuffle, suggesting the girl you have a crush on for a double. It's also the stench of shit and madacide, the misery of a zero'ing shift when you need to make rent, the insidious non-consent that hits you when your guard is down, the casual judgment from a friend at a party. For me, it was usually dangerous fun—occasionally violent, and always interesting.

Sex work defined my twenties, and continues to define my career even though I have slowly been retiring since 2013. As I did less and less sex work, I had to ask, where was Tina Horn going?

Well, I animated Tina Horn, and my clients enabled her to thrive. Yet it was my fellow sex workers that made her possible. That's why I wanted to write about them. They made the job emotionally sustainable, significantly safer from harm.

These are the stories of people who have learned how to tell you the stories you want to hear, especially the ones that hurt.

The title *Love Not Given Lightly* comes from a song by my favorite musician, Lou Reed, who died not long after I finished the first draft of this book. The song is "Venus in Furs," named for the Leopold von Sacher-Masoch novel of the same name, both of which are notorious odes to the erotics of domination and submission.

I used to play this song in session, slithering around to the pace of the tambourine, reveling in how weird it was and how much it made my clients squirm.

Maybe Lou Reed was a sadomasochist, or maybe he just enjoyed scandalizing people. Either way, Lou totally got it. He got the literary value, he got the irony, and he wrote a line that has always encapsulated both BDSM and sex work to me.

Taste the whip, in love not given lightly
Taste the whip, now bleed for me

I met the subjects of this book because we were all different kinds of professional lovers. For our clients, we provided intimacy, satisfaction, entertainment, adventure, and therapy—that kind of love. I learned early on that the best way to give what I gave at work without draining myself was to find love with my co-workers. We gave each other lust, camaraderie, support, humor, and care—that kind of love.

Being Tina Horn introduced me to myself. Being Tina Horn introduced me to many of the people who have shaped my life so far.

These are love stories. Not the love of default programming, or heteronormativity. They're stories of the way love transforms us. A transman learns to love his body. A fetishist learns to love his own cravings. A queer woman and queer man find platonic friendship as they are renting out their intimacy by the hour. An ordinary house becomes the threshold to a world of fantasy.

Being Tina Horn taught me how to love by teaching me the value of my body and my talents. It took years of actual labor for me to realize what she was trying to tell me.

You gotta labor for love. You gotta work hard to understand how love can pass through a whip, how pain can be transcendent. When you know your way around the economy of love, you know that you have to earn it.

James Darling

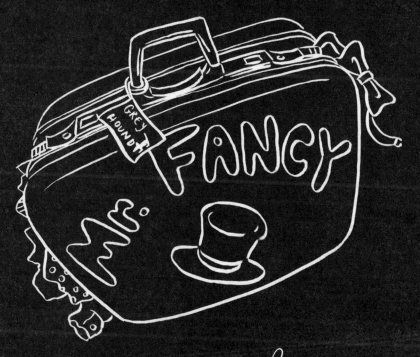

gender

"This is my sleazy porno chair," James Darling proudly tells me. Sitting before his modest Dell computer is an oversized maroon leather deck chair. To anyone else, this might just be a gaudy place to sit, but James always seems to be very clear on what possessions say about their owners.

A preternaturally calm twenty-four year old,

James has both the gravity of someone much older and the playfulness of someone much younger; he seems to be at home in this contradiction, to have almost made a fetish out of it.

It is the summer of 2012; James has been performing hardcore sex on camera for four years, mostly within the San Francisco Bay Area queer porn genre. Besides Buck Angel, he is easily the most well known **transsexual male** in the entire porn industry.

Angel, whose brand, "The Man with a Pussy," has made him one of the most famous **FTM**s in the world, period, cast James for his film *Sexing the Transman* earlier this year. It was the most mainstream porn gig someone like James could land. Once he realized he could reach audiences outside of his queer niche, James began to wonder what he could accomplish with the medium.

Thus the website *FTMFucker. com* was born. Although he is a strong voice in an international queer community that is politically outspoken on the subjects of non-traditional sexuality and

James identifies as **transsexual** because he has changed his body through hormone replacement therapy and surgery. He also identifies with the umbrella term transgender, because his gender identity differs from the sex he was assigned at birth.

FTM: A Female-to-Male trans person.

"**Cisgender**" is a term that describes a non-transgender person, from the Latin *cis* meaning "on the same side." In Latin, *trans* means "on the other side" or "across."

gender, James tells me he is less interested in making a transsexual manifesto than he is in creating "something for people to jerk off to."

At 5'9", James is often mistaken for a teenager. His nose and smile are wide, and his eyes are a dreamy bright blue. He has slender shoulders but his very short bright pink shorts are filled out with a thick round ass. Testosterone has pushed back his brown hairline and given him the wispy suggestion of a goatee. He is wearing a t-shirt I gave him that proclaims, "I'd rather be eating doughnuts than having sex," under an illustration of a pig in a dandy red robe (James is a notorious sugar fiend).

The *FTMF* teaser trailer must be finished before the Trans March on Friday. On the official first night of the world's highest-profile Gay Pride weekend, the city's transfolk and their allies congregate at Dolores Park and wind through the streets of San Francisco, protesting oppression and promoting visibility. It will be an excellent chance to spread the word about *FTMF*, which is as much *for* trans men as it is about them.

Mainstream transsexual porn exemplifies many of the more problematic qualities of the sex industry (and society, for that matter). Most companies that produce "TS" videos reduce the very existence of trans women to a fetish, using demeaning terms such as "she-male" that few trans women would use to describe themselves. In reality, there is as much diversity among trans women as there is among women who are not trans. Porn depicting trans men, realistic or no, is essentially non-existent in mainstream genres.

FTMF will be a membership site featuring trans men having hardcore sex with other trans men as well as trans women, **cisgender** men, and cisgender women. As a director, James is interested in showing trans people having the kind of exhibitionist sex they want to have. When the scenes do follow porn tropes, they're subverted with a touch of dirty camp.

Reclining in the sleazy porno chair, James cues up Final Cut Pro to show me the rough cut of the trailer. The screen flashes through the five sex scenes that have been shot for his launch. The content is far from high budget, but affordable consumer technology makes it possible for James to shoot perfectly clear, well-lit digital video.

What follows is about as no-nonsense and languid as a two-minute clip show of hardcore sex can be. I watch as two scruffy young trans guys—MJ and Charlie Spats—make out in a desk chair. The screen flashes on a curvy trans guy called Stealth Machine going down on black cis male Marlo Davis. On a sun and sweat soaked rooftop, a muscular tattooed trans guy named Billy Castro bends cis-female Bianca Stone over and fucks her with black-latex-gloved hands. Dressed as a schoolboy, James goes down on professor Ned Mayhem (cis). Audrey Rose (cis-female) goes down on James. All kinds of face slapping, oral sex, hand sex, strap-on sex, and intercourse (much of it with latex barriers) culminates in Ned ejaculating all over James.

As he watches his own cum-splattered face fade to black, James laughs and hurriedly tells me:

"I'm looking forward to having the budget to hire more people, so I don't have to put myself in every scene."

O

It's safe to say that *FTMF*'s projected fan base is not going to mind James' ubiquitous presence in this project. Onscreen and onstage, James is a natural-born sex performer, one of those people whose shyness melts away like fat sizzling off bacon when he gets hot and naked. His eyes roll back in his head as he drools over a hard cock or worships a femme. He takes a fist like a champ and he's gotta be one of the all-time best make-outs in queer porn. His appearance and demeanor are deceptively innocent, which just makes the filthy garbage that pours from his mouth that much hotter. He expertly tops with a strap-on and bottoms beautifully to hands and cocks.

It's a testament to his modesty that he chose to represent the community with which he identifies, rather than creating a vanity project. These days, most stars establish membership sites like *JoannaAngel.com* and *TS-BaileyJay.com*, capitalizing on the cult of their porno personalities. Though James could certainly get away with starting *FuckingJamesDarling.com*, he would rather help create a genre that emphasizes diverse trans men representing their sexual selves.

FTM Fucker may just supplant Buck Angel as the icon of hardcore trans masculinity simply because of its diversity of appeal. As men, the two creators couldn't be more different. Buck is a heavily tattooed, hyper-masculine body-builder. His name, face, and naked body are at the center of all of his advertising and content. James, on the other hand, describes himself as, "swishy and sparkly." An exploration of his closet says volumes about his tender, flamboyant masculinity. One could be forgiven for thinking that a fabulous drag queen, a pubescent Cub Scout, a teenage band geek, a leatherfag, and a Southern dandy shared this wardrobe. Hot Dog costumes hang next to preppy plaid shirts and strap-on harnesses.

On top of a chest of drawers, next to several vials of craft glitter, are three rubber unicorn masks. James is turning twenty-five this fall, and all he wants for his birthday is a unicorn gangbang.

🔱

If you are a trans person, you know intimately how much English fails our understanding of gender and persona. If you are cisgender, and you are skeptical of this, try writing the life story of a trans porn star.

There is a linguistic dissonance, for example, in

describing a man who was once a girl scout. Even though James does not describe himself as the kind of trans man who "always knew he was a man," it's also incorrect to use female pronouns when telling the story of his life pre-transition.

"I did have a 'girlhood,' as uncomfortable and awkward as it was, because I didn't know that I could be anything else," he says when I ask him how he would prefer I approach this issue.

We decided that I would default to male pronouns for the sake of consistency. He also approved of the language I use to describe his anatomy, such as "cock," and shifting identities such as "lesbian."

Then, there is the conundrum inherent in describing the "childhood" of "James Darling." In effect, James Darling is an artistic alter ego like Ziggy Stardust, or a public persona like the ones movie stars such as Tom Cruise have to maintain.

Let's be clear: "James Darling" is the name of a persona. The man who came up with that name, and who animates that persona, goes by another name, which is itself a different name from the one his parents gave him. Again, for the sake of consistency, I'll refer to him throughout as James.

If all of this feels strange and confusing at times, perhaps we can consider how strange and confusing it has felt to *him*.

When James was a girl, he was not the kind of girl he saw around him. When he first knew he was a man, he knew he wasn't the kind of man he saw around him either.

In Marietta, Georgia, the northern suburb of Atlanta where James was born and raised, the examples of masculinity that he saw were misogynistic. Growing up in a born-again Christian family, James was a Girl Scout and guitar player in his church band.

He was also precociously sexual; "My first memories of what sex meant to me was watching movies of teenagers in the '50s making out in cars at the drive-in. I remember coming across a copy of *The Joy of Sex* at a friend's parents' house and getting really turned on by the photos, and finding her mom's vibrators and sex toys. Eventually I would sneak every chance I could get to watch scrambled porn on the Spice channel when my parents weren't home. I was pretty stoked when I learned about AOL chatrooms and began to think Jesus looked pretty babely in a towel with blood dripping down his tortured, sinewy body. Throughout my childhood and adolescence I knew I was 'different' pretty early on—I preferred the idea of being someone's dog, unicorn, or werewolf to being someone's wife, sister or mother."

James knew he was attracted to women by puberty and identified as a lesbian by the time he was fourteen. He was never particularly butch. He rocked what he describes an "andro Annie Lennox pixie dyke look." As the only out queer person in his high school, he faced constant harassment and isolation.

"I have a theory," he says now, "that growing up in really oppressive and conservative environments just breeds stronger perverts, like trying to put out fires with gasoline."

He hooked up with girls at Girl Scout camp and youth group, until one day his father walked in on him making out with a girlfriend. Keep in mind: this was particularly upsetting because at the time, James was a teenage girl making out with another teenage girl. For the next year, his parents put him on "lock-down," and he was basically only allowed to go to church and school.

He didn't know it was possible for someone with his body to transition to male, but he loved drawing fake mustaches on his upper lip. Even as a child he vividly remembers giving himself a beard with bath bubbles. At the age of sixteen, a trans female friend introduced him to the idea of FTMs and a light bulb flipped on. He devoured the memoirs of Leslie Feinberg and Kate Bornstein, and the photography of Loren Cameron. Within the year, he had a second coming out: this time, as transgender. This is when he gave himself a new name.

At the age of nineteen, he left his parents' home to move to central Atlanta. After two years of research on options for transitioning, James decided he wanted to take hormone replacement therapy (HRT) and save for a double mastectomy, or "top surgery."

"I often ask myself: if I were stranded alone on an island, would I still need surgery? All I knew is that I would feel more comfortable moving through the world. I couldn't care less about the fact that I had a vagina. But I wanted to go swimming, be shirtless, without worrying about my chest. Top surgery became an obsession. I would spend hours doing research. I rearranged my entire life around it."

It proved very difficult to access HRT in the South. James spent a year talking to therapists and doctors trying to convince them that he wasn't too young to take testosterone. Finally he found a queer-friendly abortion clinic that agreed to prescribe his hormones. Since they didn't have a program, however, no one knew how to determine his proper dosage. For the first year of HRT, James was basically guessing how much testosterone he should be taking.

Luckily, a nurse friend who had a trans partner in the past taught James how to safely inject himself. He was taking 150 milligrams every two weeks. Later, when he moved to San Francisco and started going to a clinic called Dimensions, he learned that dosage was way too much for him. These days, he takes a much smaller dose.

The process of taking testosterone is not for the faint of heart. The hormone is suspended in cotton-seed or sesame oil, which makes it very viscous and difficult to inject. For a 150-milliliter dose like the one James started on, an 18-gauge needle is necessary.

The needle can be inserted in the thigh muscles, but it works best in the fatty tissue of the ass.

James was too intimidated to self-administer his first treatment, so he had his best friend do it. Afterwards they celebrated with champagne and cake. He was excited but he had no idea what would happen.

Over the next few years living in Atlanta, James slowly began to feel the effects of testosterone. He stopped menstruating and his voice dropped. All of a sudden, his body was totally new to him. He already had an extremely high sex drive and now he was compelled to masturbate as much as twenty times a day. He became sexually interested in men for the first time, and started hooking up with strangers he met online. This fluidity in orientation is quite common among the trans men I know; some attribute it to the appeal of gay male cruising culture, others to the expanded ideas of sexuality they experience from transitioning.

James had considered doing sex work with his roommate, another trans man. They discussed pretending to be girls and doing private sex shows for money, but they never got up the nerve. Meanwhile, an older man who responded to one of James' many Craigslist casual sex posts kept pestering him for a date. James started to wonder what it would be like to have sex with someone he wasn't attracted to, for some kind of personal gain, on his own terms. When this man suggested taking him out to dinner, James decided that he was broke and hungry enough to try it.

They went to Red Lobster, and James, "chowed down on some cheddar biscuits." The other man picked up the bill, and afterwards they had what James describes as really bad sex.

When it was over, though, he felt fine about it. He'd had sex in exchange for food. It seemed as simple as that.

⚙

During this time, James became interested in Atlanta's underground performance scene. The first burlesque act he ever saw was Vagina Jenkins, a voluptuous black performer who brought a modern queer sensibility to classic vaudeville. Her group the Dixie Pistols put on raunchy shows in bars, which the eighteen-year-old James had to sneak into.

"I was so floored by the beauty of these women," he says, sighing. "Their grace, their poise, their costumes, their attention to detail. I'd never seen anyone express their sexuality in such an open and public way."

James was so taken with this theatrical world that he was soon begging to be involved. They smuggled him into the scene—first as an assistant, and later onstage.

That's James Darling for you. He wants to go where he wants to go, and he'll find a way to charm himself inside.

Failing that, he'll hop the fence.

Soon, Vagina invited him to do a number with her and another female performer named Camilla Cuntwell. The Dixie Pistols loved the gender-bending conceit of an FTM drag king: a man, assigned female at birth, dressing as a woman pretending to be a man. Though James had done a little bit of drag in his youth group (his first act, to the Cure song "Boys' Don't Cry," didn't go over well with the pop-loving Christian teens), this was the first time he'd ever taken off his clothes in front of an audience.

"It was the most exhilarating thing I'd ever done, having that attention on me. To be seen as this masculine being, seduced by beautiful femmes onstage, triggered my love of exhibitionism. I'd fucked girlfriends in semi-public spaces like graveyards and playgrounds before. But that performance was the first time it was intentional for people to see me in a sexual way."

His dapper stage persona developed a small local following and he took on the name Mr. Fancy. Vagina encouraged and mentored him, introducing him to the concept of "boylesque"—men doing glamorous stripteases. James was discovering how to market himself as his own kind of man and people were responding.

"This has been a theme in my life. How do I make

who I know myself to be something that people will enjoy seeing and want to pay for, and still remain true to who I am?"

While searching for a gig bag, James found a thrift-store hard-shell red vintage suitcase with a pink satin interior. He covered it with rhinestones and emblazoned it with the words "Mr. Fancy" in glittery silver paint.

This was one of two pieces of luggage he took with him when, in 2009, he moved to San Francisco on a Greyhound bus, seeking new queer frontiers.

§

Like Joe Buck in *Midnight Cowboy*, James set out for the big city with fantastic dreams, no real plan, and very little money in his pocket. But he had been on a few trips to the Bay Area for **Leather community** conferences, where he'd met a boy named Cyd who was also early in his transition.

James was just starting to get on his feet in the Bay, stringing together food service jobs, when Cyd asked if he was interested in shooting a hardcore video for a website called *Crash Pad Series*. The pay was $200 for a few hours' work, and James couldn't think of a reason to say no.

Leather Community: kink subcultures, often queer, many of which grew out of regional motorcycle clubs.

CPS is an episodic porn membership site directed by a queer black female filmmaker named Shine Louise Houston. It has a very simple conceit: a camera is "hidden" in a crash pad where queers come to have sex. The performers are given very little direction, and encouraged to show off unconventional acts and bodies. Though the cinematography and editing are very stylized, the resulting scenes feel more like documentary than a porn production.

To watch James's first porn scene with Cyd on *CPS* is to watch two people coming into their own both as performers and as men. They play out a high school jock role-play in which Cyd has bound James in rope to punish him for some homophobic comments. The baby fat of their queerness is showing. The word "faggot" is used as both intimidation and encouragement. Cyd is cocky, bossy, and sure of himself in his role as intimidator. James is more timid. His Southern accent is pronounced. His eyes waver in and out of focus, of character. Every so often he gets a defiant word in.

James was amazed by how comfortable he was shooting sex for *CPS*. The crewmembers respected his pronouns and were visibly moved by his coming-out story in the Behind the Scenes interview. He invented the name James Darling for this shoot, in tribute to his Southern dandy roots, to Warhol Superstar Candy Darling, and the trans female porn star Gia Darling.

"I walked away from that experience feeling like I wanted to do this all the time. This is so much fun!

I get to fuck somebody I'm really into. As shy as I've always been I've always enjoyed public attention around sex," he says.

By the next year, James would be given his chance to break into the porn scene. But first he needed to get grounded in San Francisco. So he started escorting.

There are several ways for Bay Area sex workers to find clients. A site called *ErosGuide.com* charges $50 for an ad. It has a sophisticated design and is very careful about the way it represents its providers in order to leap through legal loopholes. **MyRedBook.com** is free and has a much simpler user interface. Craigslist is also an option, although the management will take down anything they perceive to be illegal.

Eros tends to attract sex tourists and businessmen with more money to spend, and men for whom hiring sex workers is a regular pastime. Redbook is more for dabblers, for a consumer who has an itch to scratch. Craigslist attracts the most impulsive and naive clients.

James got tips and advice on breaking into sex work from many of the new friends he was making in San Francisco. There was less of a social stigma against it than he had experienced in the South. In fact, there was an emerging

MyRedBook.com was shut down by the FBI in 2014.

culture of pride and support among young people choosing to escort, dance, or provide fetish services.

Though by his own admission he didn't always make the best decisions, he felt supported by his sex worker friends: "I knew enough to let someone know where I was going and when to expect me back."

James placed an ad in the transsexual sections of these sites, attracting clients who claimed to be bi-curious or bisexual. In the female fetish section, he advertised as a tomboy lesbian. Even though he had been injecting testosterone for several years and his voice had dropped a few registers, he still hadn't grown much hair. His clitoris had grown to two inches and he still had considerable 36DD breasts. His particular androgyny piqued the curiosity of his ostensibly straight male customers. Clothed, James was easily read as male. Naked, his breasts and vagina appealed to a heterosexual desire.

At first, James would ask his clients what inspired them to come see him, trying to gauge whether his trans body was an asset. Soon he realized that the question was anxiety provoking and diminished return business. Like any industry, repeat clients are highly desirable for a sex worker, so James learned to stifle his curiosity.

That first year, James worked relentlessly. He met men at the Hot Tubs, a business that rents private rooms with Jacuzzis and saunas for $30 an hour. During a period when he could arrange to see five clients a day, he would host them in a cheap hotel room. For a while he ran in-calls out of his apartment in the Sunset district while his roommates were at work.

He says that much of that time was a blur, but some clients stand out. He had a regular who worked as a construction worker. "I felt like I was living every gay man's fantasy, gettin' plowed on top of some power tools, sawdust stickin' to my ass," he describes it.

The subject of his gender sometimes caused confusion, but he says he wasn't personally offended if his clients thought of him as a woman. In effect, he was renting out a female body from which he felt totally dissociated.

"I was not in my body. I felt—'Here's this body that people are willing to pay for. Take it. This doesn't really feel like a part of me.' It was not triggering that people were paying for my tits. 'You want these tits? You can have them. They're nice tits. They'd be nicer on somebody else.'" He imitates the thought-process of his former self as he says this, scooping and pushing away the phantom breasts of his now-flat chest.

His low voice on the phone was often a giveaway that he wasn't simply a tomboy. Occasionally he would get people who were specifically looking for a trans man, like the middle-aged lesbian couple that hired him to clean their house naked.

James admits that his boundaries weren't so good at the time. "I basically let people do whatever they wanted as long as there was a condom on it. I just wanted their money and for it to be over and to move on."

He worked with little regard for his own self-care. One day when he had a cold he did an intense blowjob scene; suffice to say there was snot, spit, and tears flying everywhere.

All the while, he was putting money away to save for the thing he wanted most in life: top surgery, to remove his biggest moneymakers.

I met James in the fall of 2009 when we were both cast in a full-length porn movie called **Bordello.** It was the second or third porno gig either of us had ever had. The sex toy retailer Good Vibrations had contracted several directors to shoot sex-positive, queer, kinky, unconventional films, and local sex professionals were getting a ton of work.

Carson, Akira Raine and I played cigar-chomping johns who show up at the bordello of the title just in time for a murder mystery. An ensemble of other sex workers, including James, played the whores. The Madame's servant is found dead. Everyone has to figure out if the killer used the dagger, the rope, a candle; you can probably guess what we used them for instead.

I knew I would like James as soon as I saw how much theatricality he brought to this madcap set. He wore a tuxedo shirt with the sleeves cut off, the white cuffs preserved as bracelets, a black vest, sock garters, and shiny shorts. He generously lent me a royal blue ascot, dandifying my own costume considerably. During our three-way with Vid Tuesday, he also wore a steel butt plug with a shiny gem visible in its base. In another scene, with Carson, he fellated a real pistol like it was the hottest cock he had ever had in his mouth.

He considers this controversial gun scene to be the moment his career really took off. Using Facebook, Twitter, and Tumblr, he began connecting with his growing fan base. He started getting a lot of messages from people who appreciated his representation of trans men.

In *Bordello*, as with many of his early scenes, he either bound his breasts with a black binder or let them hang out from a vest. James says he was proud to show his transition on camera over several years, insisting, "Trans men are men no matter how much surgery they've had."

Still, surgery is what drove him. Eventually he saved up the money to reconstruct his chest.

In April of 2010, James flew to Baltimore to see a doctor who had agreed to give him a deal on top surgery. That same day, he went under the knife.

"Unless you're there, it's very hard to understand the desire to have a body you can live in. Your body doesn't feel whole. You feel outside of it."

One afternoon, not long after we met on the *Bordello* set, but before he flew to Baltimore, James boarded a bus I was riding down 24th Street in San Francisco's Mission District. He wore black slacks and a buttoned up blue dress shirt with a blazer. I caught his attention, and his eyes lit up as he made his way up the aisle to me. When I asked him what he was up to, he replied without hesitation:

"I was seeing a client."

Pulling with both hands, almost hanging, on the straps that dangle from the bus ceiling, James gave me the little conspiratorial smirk of a kid who has several bills in his pocket because he knows how to market himself.

I had inadvertently caught him during one of the best moments in sex work: the moment of victory, of pulling it off. He was on his way home to his Mission apartment and then out to meet friends, like all the other working stiffs on that bus. A combination of talent, luck, and audacity had come together that night so he could afford a burrito, some beers, bus fare, rent, and eventually the funds to reconstruct his body.

James returned to the world of San Francisco porn literally a new man. I had started directing for a site I co-created called *QueerPorn.TV*. We cast James in one of his first post-surgery scenes, bottoming to cis male

Wolf Hudson on a sunny afternoon in the skylight-covered **bathtub** of my Oakland apartment. He continued to perform for local sites like *CPS* and *Heavenly Spire*, and model for print magazines such as *Original Plumbing*, proudly showing off his flat chest. I ran into him dancing in the streets at the Dyke March that June, colorful rhinestones appliquéd to his still-red scars; he told me he was on top of the world.

Escorting, however, would never be the same. Clients could no longer fool themselves into believing that they were having sex with a woman. As James points out:

"When it comes to the adult industry, what I've discovered is you need to have tits or a dick, or people just aren't interested because they don't understand what's sexual about your body."

So James picked up two part-time gigs. He refers to them as his "straight" jobs, though they were both sex-adjacent. The first was working as a receptionist at Eros, a men's bathhouse in San Francisco's Castro District. The other was assisting *Kink.com*'s live cam site. Both jobs involved mopping up cum and being in highly sexualized environments: all the grime, none of the glory.

Tubs are actually very unforgiving places to have sex, but he and Wolf were champs and the resulting scene is a classic of the genre if I do say so myself.

Without the goal of top surgery to drive him, James became increasingly depressed.

"People say sex work kills your sex life," he says in retrospect. "My straight jobs destroyed me more than sex work ever did."

In early 2012, he reached a breaking point and quit the *Kink.com* job. He had wanted to start his own site devoted to trans men for years. So with the money he had saved, he spent five months developing *FTMFucker.com*.

"The thing that's liberating about making content for *FTFM* is that almost everything involving trans men in porn has never been seen before. "

The Feminist Porn Awards have been held every April in Toronto, Ontario since 2006. Run by an independent sex toy retailer called Good For Her, the FPAs are to the Adult Video News Awards roughly what the Independent Spirit Awards are to the Oscars. The FPAs celebrate porn that foregrounds female orgasms, compassionate BDSM, queer sex acts like fisting, and transgender performers.

In April 2012, I traveled with James and a sizable crew of San Francisco queer porn stars to Toronto for the FPAs. The Awards Gala is in a church, and that church is filled with glamorous people in leather, latex, plunging décolletage, and towering heels. Categories honor educational films, representations of bisexuality, and diversity in casting while long clips from the nominees play onscreen.

During the screening, I slipped out of the audience for a bathroom break.

In the mezzanine ladies' room, I was gossiping and reapplying lip-gloss when I heard a loud moan from the theater.

"Is that James?" I asked out loud.

I dashed out of the bathroom, across the foyer, past the balcony seats. There, on the film screen, was a video of James Darling, masturbating.

I put my elbows on the balcony and leaned in to intently watch this scene from *Sexing the Transman*. The film was shot in HD and James' crotch was in crisp focus. The scene was basically one long close-up of James fucking and rubbing himself to orgasm. His brow furrowed in ecstasy. He pulled on his dick and muttered, "I'm so close!"

Later in the evening, James would be awarded Heartthrob of the Year, honoring the visibility he brings to trans male sexuality.

That visibility is sometimes manifested a little too literally for one guy to handle. Peering down into the audience below, I could see James himself, in a suit and tie, in the second row. The guy whose genitals were being projected twenty-two feet tall for five hundred people, the guy with the sleazy porno chair, the guy who has transformed his identity into his livelihood, was shrinking into his seat, trying to disappear.

The
Gates

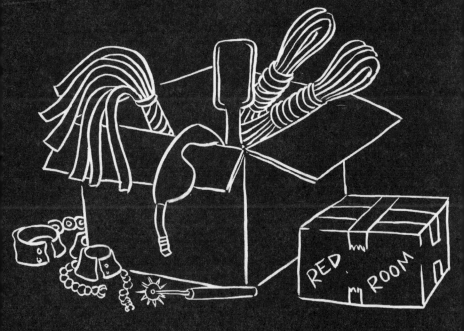

RED ROOM

community

The Gates

In 2013, if you are in the Bay Area and you are looking to hire a lady for any number of fetish services, the first thing that you are likely to do is to look at the listings on *ErosGuide.com*. Browsing through the thumbnails, you will see asses framed by garter belts, a lot of cleavage busting out of vinyl bustiers, and many different kinds of feminine faces staring intently back at you. Among the names of women who work independently—Lucinda Archer, Selina Raven, Colette—you will see several houses: Fantasy Makers, the English Mistress, and the Gates.

The Gates' thumbnail depicts a woman in a tight black dress shoving another woman against a St Andrew's Cross and threatening her with a paddle. Click on it, and an ad appears with eight smaller thumbnails representing a variety of the house's current crop of women.

The ad states:

The Gates has been open continuously since 1994, in the same safe, discreet and convenient location a short 20 minutes outside of downtown San Francisco.

Our home currently offers five lavishly equipped session rooms featuring a very wide array of equipment and devices, and each room has a distinct theme and ambiance, ranging from the Rubber Executive Dungeon - a formal and severely elegant space, to the Boudoir - a gentle and comfortable setting.

Stunning as our home and facilities are, they cannot compare to the breathtaking beauty of the women of The Gates. A brief glimpse at our website will introduce you to the physical appeal of our staff, and when you meet us in person you will be delighted by the wit, charm, creativity, grace and individuality you will discover in each of the ladies.

Here are a few of the many advantages we have to offer over others in our field:

· *We are here when it's convenient for you - open seven days a week from 10am until 10pm, available in as little as thirty minutes from the time of your call.*
· *We have a large staff body and several people available at all times, allowing you both variety in the selection of the person or people you see, as well as making ever-popular group or "party" sessions an option without hassle or delay.*
· *Our ladies are of all different experience levels, body types, ages and ethnic backgrounds, giving you the opportunity to find the exact match for your preferences.*
· *Our differently-themed rooms make it possible for you to enact your fantasy in the setting that is most exciting to you.*
· *We are very competitively priced compared to many "independents" who offer services that are virtually identical to ours.*
· *We are happy to accept credit cards.*
· *We have established an excellent reputation in the community during our over seventeen years of service due to our ongoing efforts to provide you with a safe, clean, discreet, well-equipped and, most of all, fun and fabulous place to play.*

Give us a call today to arrange your session,
and we look forward to playing with you!

There is a link to a website, and a phone number to call. The Gates' site has a simple red on black design. In their pictures, the women are dressed in leather boots, latex bras, vinyl corsets, or satin lingerie. Some show their faces, some show their breasts. Some emphasize their feet, some their asses, some their dominance, some their masochism. They are mostly white, slender, and in their 20's. There are a few Asian ladies, a few black ladies, and a few that are curvier than the others.

If you call the number, you will be greeted by a single word; "Hello."

In the early 1990's, while grunge music was glamorizing the darkness of the modern soul, when the obscene details of the American president's sex life were international news, a barely legal young woman in Oakland, California learned that there was good money to be made dressing in leather and subjecting men to exquisite torture.

This woman, who would eventually take on the name Sage Travigne, was nineteen years old when her friend's godmother asked her if she knew anything about bondage.

"I had tried it with my boyfriends," she says now, "but I didn't know it was *bondage*."

The friend knew of a "playhouse" a few miles east of Oakland that employed young women to see clients for something called "fantasy and fetish exploration." Sage was unquestionably attractive and naturally bossy. The prospect of making money off those qualities was very appealing; so was the idea of quitting her job as an assistant for disabled folks, where she knew she would never get a raise. Though she didn't quite understand what this new job would entail, the style and attitude seemed compatible with her love of heavy metal and sexy shoes.

So Sage took the BART out to El Cerrito and interviewed with the house's "coordinator," Lorette. She was soon installed at Fantasy Makers.

Her first client was a foot fetishist and she had absolutely no idea what to do with him, but after a few sessions she began to realize she was a natural. The work suited her. The way Fantasy Makers was run, however, did not. Nothing was designed in a way that made Sage feel sexy, and she didn't like the way Lorette condescended to her.

Eventually she moved to another house called the Shadows, which had better facilities but presented other problems. The owner of the Shadows shamelessly slept with his employees. Sage found it equally offensive that he charged the working ladies for sodas and snacks.

After nearly two years of working for others,

Sage decided she had learned enough about clients to run her own operation. She rented a small apartment on Woolsey Street in Berkeley and took out an ad in *Spectator* magazine. She got male friends to do security. Eventually she had so many clients trying to book her, she began to wish she could be in two places at once. That led to her inviting other female friends to take sessions out of her space. When she realized she was running an organization, she decided to give it a name with an appropriate mystique: The Gates.

The early days of the Gates were a lot of fun for dommes and clients alike, but the whole thing would have certainly collapsed after a few exciting months if it wasn't for Sage's natural talent for order and accountability.

"Every rule at the Gates is based on a reaction to something that I didn't like about other people I worked for," she says.

When business continued to improve, she rented an even larger house in Oakland. This place, which she now calls The First Big House, had enough space that she and her then-boyfriend Mark could build unique wooden bondage structures. With the extra money that was coming in she invested in more furniture, nicer gear, and bigger ads.

By January 2006, Sage employed around twenty women. At mandatory monthly meetings, they addressed interpersonal conflicts, and collectively brainstormed how the house could run more effectively.

At one such meeting, Sage had a surprise for her

employees: "Well, ladies, the good news is, we're not having a meeting tonight because I just bought the house across the street!"

There were cheers. The only thing a collective loves more than a meeting is no meeting.

"The bad news is; you're all helping move right now!"

There were groans.

So in the early winter evening, twenty-some plainclothes dominatrixes hauled boxes marked "Executive" and "Blue Room" and filled with leather, rubber, wood, metal and linens across 57th street to the New Big House, where The Gates has operated ever since.

In cut-off jean shorts and cotton tank tops, Sage is every bit the California golden girl. She has a slender, athletic build, with well-proportioned breasts and hips and a clear, tanned face. Her hair is auburn-colored, and her eyes are icy blue. She is vegetarian and fond of Newcastle beer. Even when she is being silly, which is often, she possesses an unwavering solemnity. When she puts together an outfit from her stunning closet of fetish gear, that calm demeanor, along with tight rubber corsets and six-inch black stilettos, holds her body high and proud.

Nowadays it would be an understatement to describe Sage as someone who understands bondage. At the age of thirty-nine she has been managing The Gates for nearly twenty years. Of all the kinky things she has learned to do, tying people up remains her favorite. She has grown from an opportunistic teen-ager with a penchant for thigh-high boots to one of the Bay Area commercial BDSM scene's most established bosses.

Though she no longer takes sessions, Sage continues to teach the difference between a square knot and a granny knot to countless young women who are curious, as she once was, about this particular kind of sex work, and who want to learn about it in a woman-friendly environment.

In 2006, I was one such woman. I worked for Sage first on staff and later as a "right hand man" manager, for four years. No other experience has changed the course of my life so completely.

It's 9:30am on a Wednesday in mid-June and the morning shift is arriving at Oakland's premier house of BDSM.

In a sense, "The Big House"—as it's known to the ladies who work there—is the actual two-story Victorian house, which—due to careful soundproofing and window boarding—blends in with the other homes in its working-class neighborhood. "The Gates" is more of an abstract place, a state of mind. It is, as the name implies, a threshold. Through this opening, you may, for the price of admission, enter a world in which it is possible for your erotic fantasies to become real.

Some employees arrive by car, some by bicycle. Some walk from the nearby BART station. Some women's partners drop them off, and some spring for cabs. Sage is a dog owner, and allows her workers to bring theirs to work, so there is usually a motley pack lounging behind the tall wooden fence of the backyard.

The coworkers greet one another enthusiastically. Morale is high. Autumn, who has long straight brown hair and a bombshell figure poured into a white velvet tracksuit, is the manager today. She grabs a clipboard off a nail in the kitchen wall and begins to assign tasks.

"Cielo, can you do inventory? Louise I know you like to sweep. I'll take care of the recycling and the rubber wall polishing."

After greeting her employees, Sage settles herself at her office desk with a meticulously organized date book and a pint glass of steaming herbal tea.

The other women, who range in age from precocious eighteen to a very well preserved forty year old, get straight to work without complaining. If there is a prima donna among them she does not take this moment to reveal herself. Dishes are put away and the whistling kettle is taken off the stove. Yards of cotton rope are pulled out of the dryer and coiled. When the chores are done, the women settle down at the kitchen table with black coffee and bottles of kombucha to discuss, along with their outrageous sexual exploits, life's more mundane subjects like television, children, and car trouble.

These routines are the only action in the house for about half an hour. Then, the phone rings.

The answering tension emanating from the ladies in the kitchen is palpable through the entire house. They have been trained to answer the phone before the fourth ring, and to put aside anything they might be doing—cooking breakfast, painting nails, doing homework—to prioritize the phone. On the other end of the line is the potential for money. Regardless of their individual motivations, money is what they're all here for.

This is a business, after all.

"Hello," Sage says, in a voice just a few registers below her usual speaking tone. She doesn't say, "Thank you for calling the Gates," or, "This is Sage," or, "How can I help you?" Her phone voice has a cool, emotionless femme-fatale quality. It's not the accommodating chirp of a perky secretary or the alluring tone of a phone-sex operator. Sage means business on the phone. She does not believe in flirting to get clients to book. She doesn't "give free phone sessions."

Sage asks the client what he's interested in. She keeps the conversation focused on availability, times, and other practical concerns. When he arrives, the client will have a chance to discuss more intimate details with the woman he books.

The price starts at $160 for an hour, and is referred to as a "Donation." It is non-negotiable. The rate increases, with up-sell craftiness, to $220 for 90 minutes, $280 for two hours, and so on through overnight sessions. Adding a second lady to your scene costs an extra hundred an hour. Adding a lady for a "walk-on" or cameo appearance is $20 for ten minutes, $40 for twenty, $50 for a half an hour. Bringing another lady in for a golden shower is 20 even if it takes less than ten minutes.

Some people call the Gates because they have a very specific fantasy they can't get off their mind. Many imagine that if the fantasy were consummated it will lose its obsessive hold. Sometimes this works and sometimes it doesn't.

Some clients are hobbyists. For them spanking is like tennis and bondage is like cooking class. These people consider themselves connoisseurs of an experience, and of the professional ladies themselves.

Some clients are enchanted by the general idea of dark, cruel women, of non-normative sexuality. Some of these people have no idea what they're getting themselves into.

Some clients are looking for a mistress for an ongoing professional relationship, the way that other people might search for a good stylist, personal trainer, or therapist.

Some clients want to lie on their back while a woman literally walks all over them. Some of them want something in their mouths. Some want to be locked in a closet and ignored. Some want to be completely mummified in saran wrap. Some want the surface of their skin pierced with 24-gauge needles. Some want a gallon of water sprayed up their rectum with a shower nozzle. Some want to be called slave, slut, dog, whore, toy, butt-boy, worm, scum, or pathetic worthless cum dumpster.

Some arrive with scripts, with duffle bags of personal toys, with outfits for themselves, with outfits for their mistress.

Some want somebody to talk to.

4

When you book a session at the Gates, you arrive right on time. You ring the bell, and step through the front door to a glass-walled porch filled with potted houseplants. The door to the house swings open, and you enter.

Behind the door stands the lady you've booked your session with. She ushers you into a living room and sits you down on an enormous comfortable black leather couch. On the coffee table before you are some large hardcover books of fetish photographers Erik Kroll and Doris Kloster. To your left, freshwater fish swim in an enormous tank.

Your mistress sits opposite you on another, smaller couch. She may be in a dress, or robe, but she is not naked or in fetish gear. One of the rules of the house is that negotiation is conducted between two consenting adults with as little distraction as possible. Regardless of whatever depraved roles you may eventually play, this is a professional discussion.

She smiles, and greets you with pleasantries, like an old friend or a hairdresser. Then she gets down to business. What are you in the mood for today? What's your fantasy? What are your turn-ons? What are you curious about, and what is an absolute boundary? Do you have specific attire requests? Are you interested in a walk-on from another lady? There may be a new girl in training: how would you feel about her sitting in on session?

Your mistress might ask you about any safety concerns you have. Can you be on your knees for long periods of time? How's your heart?

She suggests you "get business out of the way" and you hand her a bank envelope, or a gift bag, or a sweaty wad of bills. She retreats with a smile behind a thick black curtain to an unseen room. For a few minutes you wait, wring your hands, stare at the fish, or flip through an art book. Your heart thumps and your imagination runs wild.

Behind the curtain is the world you don't see.

Sometimes the woman who walks through that curtain becomes another person when she's not putting on a show for you. The glamour melts away, replaced by conspiratorial winks, or weariness. Sometimes the woman is the same whether she is arriving, sweeping the floors, or flogging a naked man.

There are people who would probably pay good money just to be chained up so they could silently observe this backstage area: the office, the kitchen, the locker room basement, and the back porch. But that is not on the menu. Though countless scenes can be created within these walls, the world on the other side of the black curtain is one to which no amount of money can permit you access.

After what seems like an eternity, your mistress returns, and probably says something commanding like, "Follow me," or something cute like, "Right this way to your doom!"

1

You can learn a lot about someone based on how they react to the news that you're working as a professional dominatrix. Upon learning that I loved this mysterious job, my old pal Lucas mused, "If I had the money to go to that house, I'd hire all the girls for the night and we'd all get naked and just do something totally ordinary . . . like order a pizza!"

My mother asked, "What's a dominatrix?"

And my friend Jason said: "Good. You're going to learn a lot about men."

What Jason had wrong is that being a sex worker merely confirmed everything I already knew quite well about men. Clients, with all their wildly diverse ages, classes, ethnicities, values, manners, and desires, have always been a snap for me.

What I never expected to learn through working in a bondage house was how to love women.

Sage created something I had never been a part

of before: a place where powerful females supported one another to get the project of making money done safely and efficiently. The Gates is a rare business in which all the workers are female and—with one or two notable exceptions—all the customers are male.

While we were working at the Gates, we weren't only powerful because we were the ones holding the ropes and the crops (although that literalization of dynamics certainly helps drive the point home). We were powerful because we were women who guided men into sexual discovery. Both clients and workers learned things about themselves in session, but it was the ladies who were the guardians of the mystique.

Men entered, and made themselves more vulnerable to strangers than they did to anyone else in their lives. Then they left, all without knowing the first thing about how the house was run. For the most part, they were like fine diners who arrive at a restaurant without ever considering what goes on in the kitchen.

Certainly, some clients thought we all just materialized, corsets cinched, as soon as they wanted us. That we were never tired, or feeling unsexy. That we never got colds.

The truth, of course, is that someone was always rushing to lace up her boots, and someone was always complaining about her numbers, and sometimes we just sat around all afternoon waiting for the phone to ring.

We all had different motivations for being there

and we didn't always see eye to eye. But there was a reason we all worked in a house instead of going solo. When a girl went into session, she knew she wasn't alone.

Because whether she'd had five Steve's that day or only one half-hour golden shower, or whether she'd been sling height and elbow deep in a middle-aged man, or been rubbed down in baby oil, whether he'd respected her dignity or she'd spent two hours batting greedy hands away, whether she felt very powerful or very small, whether she'd forgotten her troubles or been reminded of them, whether she'd been a schoolgirl or a satanic nun or a cuckolding wife, whether she'd been pretending not to watch the clock, or finding herself being strangely turned on by creepy "Uncle Mike" who talks like Jack Nicholson—she could eventually kick off her heels and unzip her leather, collapse in laughter or burst into tears. She knew that these women, whether in sweats or cock-tail dresses or lacy panties or nothing at all were there for her—to break the spell, to help her stain another coffee mug or champagne flute with red lip prints, to commiserate and corroborate and remind her that she was real.

What struck me most about working for Sage was how much it reminded me of my best experiences with cooperative living. The decency of the house's rules made it possible for women to make good money working outside of established commercial systems that often oppress them or limit their options. The careful attention to safety concerns made it possible for clients to survive more abstract, psychological danger.

In my time there, I learned enormous amounts of practical kink skills like bondage tricks and the proper way to choke someone out. I also learned profound things about the human sexual imagination. The most important of these is the role that irony plays in fantasy: the dark, depraved, degrading scenes that are commissioned around the clock at the Gates are predicated on respect and clear communication. The implied meaning of a scene is most often the opposite of the literal meaning.

At the Gates, sex is dressed up in darkness but I have never been around so many giggles, so much emotional catharsis, so much evident healing.

When playing at the Gates, you have five choices of environment. Across from the negotiation room is the Executive Dungeon. Here, the ceiling is painted a muted gold. The walls are made of black rubber. On one wall is a wooden St Andrew's cross and in the corner is a leather-upholstered spanking bench. In the center of the space is the house's most impressive and unique piece of furniture: a stainless steel bed with hooks all up and down its four posters. This room is elegant, understated despite its scandalous setting. A wooden suspension bar hangs from a rig in the ceiling. Every room, in fact, has one of these rigs, and each one can support a 300-pound man.

The boudoir is next door. Painted a lively green, it contains a matching white IKEA bed, vanity and wardrobe. Inside the wardrobe are size thirteen high-heeled shoes, enormous panties, pantyhose, and costume makeup. This room is suitable for domestic scenes, cross dressing, or sensual sessions that involve oral worship of a lady's feet, legs, ass, or breasts (never, it must be emphasized, her vagina or anus, and it is extremely rare for a lady to kiss on the mouth). It also attracts clients who have physical limitations and need to spend most of the session sitting or lying down.

Through the foyer and up the hardwood stairs is the house's top floor. The office/schoolroom is first, containing a wooden desk large enough for a small person to lie flat on his or her stomach, a small linen couch, and—somewhat incongruously for the setting—another leather spanking bench. Role-plays involving school or work or doctor's offices are very common, because these are primal places for power dynamics to manifest.

Next is the Blue Room or Worship Room in which there is another wooden cross, a man-sized cage with a leather table for a top and a closet converted into an iron jail cell. The midnight blue of the walls and numerous mirrors make the place seem much more cavernous than its true dimensions.

Lastly, the red room is draped floor to ceiling in red curtains that evoke the nightmare scenes of *Twin Peaks* combined with a warmly erotic Parisian bordello. A wooden structure designed for all kinds of bondage dominates the space, though somehow there is also room for a leather futon and wooden riding horse with real equestrian saddle.

Every room contains the following items: a spray bottle of madacide (medical-grade disinfectant), water-based lubricant, at least ten condoms, several carabineers, some kind of bondage cuffs, several coils of cotton rope, at least one flogger, a Wartenberg wheel, a blindfold, a collar, a leash, metal nipple clamps, a collection of clothespins, tea light candles and votives, a box of matches, and an assortment of intimidating dildos.

The other doors on the second floor lead to: a linen supply closet filled with lube, towels, sheets, and enema bags; the bathroom, which contains a bathtub for golden and brown showers (the only room in the house with a window that isn't frosted or boarded over); and, the upstairs apartment where Sage used to live. Trusted friends inhabit the apartment; it is the only space in the entire house that is not designated as The Gates. A stereo blasts punk music in that apartment all day to muffle the sounds of mundane life: without noise pollution, someone in the Red Room can hear everything that goes on in the next room, and vice versa.

Regardless of which room you chose, what

happens when you enter is between you and your mistress.

When I closed the session room door behind me, I would always order my submissive client to strip, fold up his clothes and get down on his knees, forehead pressed to the floor. He probably never imagined that this domineering goddess had swept the room that morning wearing basketball shorts.

Then, I would stalk around him, taking my time, savoring the *click clack* of my heels on hardwood. Dramatically, I would slap my own hand with a riding crop in time to my burned cd copy of Charles Mingus' *Black Saint and the Sinner Lady*. I'd drag the crop along his exposed back, raising his hair and goosebumps and reminding him that he was surrendering himself to me.

The first thing I always asked a client was, "What was the last thing you jerked off to?" or, "What did you think about when you first started masturbating?" I asked because it made them delightfully uncomfortable, but mostly I asked because I wanted to know. Those secrets fed me and filled me up.

I was so lucky to have—and I'm not pretending to be the first drama-queer-turned-whore to say this—the best-paid improv gig in town. More than being a dominatrix, I was a highly valued, living, breathing storytelling machine. Part of the reason this worked was that I was fueled, not drained, by the stories my clients wanted me to tell them, and the stories they gave me in return.

During my four years of working shifts at the Gates, and later when I went independent, renting dungeon studios from other women, I did sometimes embody the stereotype of a dominatrix.

I spoke in a sinister velvet purr to a revolving door of strange men. I tied a hundred thousand half hitches and said the word "bad" enough for a lifetime. Men looked at me with fear and desire and coughed up their cash, which I used to buy red meat, red wine, BART fare, bike tubes, custom guitars, comic books, and one round-trip plane ticket to Brazil. Some of the things I said on the clock were objectively dark, I suppose. But the darkness never followed me out the door. On the contrary, I always left work feeling elated, the way I do after watching, say, a David Cronenberg movie. I looked depravity in the face and the world never stopped turning.

My curiosity took me pretty far, as did my tolerance for strong smells. I interrogated and I teased. I smothered men's faces with my ass, admiring my own made-up face in the mirror as I counted the moments until I would allow him to breathe again. I covered my arms in latex veterinarian gloves and stuck myself elbow deep into the all-too-willing rectum of a sixty-year-old man, pumping him to countless shuddering internal orgasms. I electrocuted and pierced scrotums, bound them in cotton rope until they were purple, seemingly ready to pop, and then kicked them with my Pleaser pumps as hard as I possibly could.

Men brought toys to share, devices they had found or made and cherished for decades. Some of them brought scripts and some expected me to intuit what they needed. I locked them in closets, cages, and leather hoods.

I humiliated men for their penis size, relative to the size of my imaginary boyfriend, ridiculing them for never being able to satisfy me with that sorry excuse for a dick. I threatened to throw my client in the back of a van and drive up and down Polk Street, using him to make some extra cash. I dressed them in negligees and feather boas and instructed them to walk in kitten heels. I gave them lessons in femininity that I myself had only recently learned.

I was a jukebox of hits: a lusty space alien, an exploited babysitter, a naïve niece, a sultry librarian, a specialized therapist, the captain of a slave ship, a corrupt governess, and a bossy lesbian girlfriend. I said the most facile sentences imaginable and watch a man's eyes roll back in his head in ecstasy.

Men have swallowed my coffee piss and beer spit, licked my sweaty feet and choked on my strap-on cock.

I once fucked my gorgeous coworker with my hands while a client poured cheap chardonnay all over us, ruining the sheets.

On one glorious day, I kicked open the door,

strode into the room, and decked a man in the face with a key lime pie.

Yet all of these scenes, everything my clients and I negotiated, were no more the point of the Gates than the plot of a movie is the point of a multiplex. The point was that a woman created a business and a bunch of other women helped her to run it.

For most of my twenties, being a dominatrix was my job, my choice, my danger, and my life. Since I was a teenager, I had made money lots of different ways. Barista. Boardwalk clerk. Pizza place manager. Head shop receiver. Marketing intern. Magazine intern. *Actual* babysitter. I worked in a recycling center collecting cans from drifters. I sat at a desk and wrote copy about fine wine, pretending I wasn't spending most of my shift making lists about bands on Myspace.

"Professional Dominatrix," as flamboyant as it sounds, was the first completely sensible job I ever had. I suspect I will never work a job more sensible. The exchange of labor, time, and wage always felt exactly correct.

At the end of a sesson, when a client was putting his street clothes on, he often asked me: "What's your favorite part about being a dominatrix?"

Of course I usually told him that it was the glamour, the clothes, the chance to control men, something about female supremacy.

In reality, my favorite part was always the part where they give me their money.

Only once did I ever make the mistake of trying to spend the night alone at the Gates.

I was living in San Francisco and commuting to the East Bay every weekend to work the Friday evening and Saturday morning shifts. This was right before the 2008 recession and my business was unbelievable. I saw four to five clients a day on average. In the space of eight hours or so I easily did more sexual experimentation than most humans will do in a lifetime.

On these shifts, I worked myself up into ecstatic states of concentration and completely forgot that the rest of the world with its formalities of politeness even existed. Fueled by pure fantasy, I rarely had time to eat. About twenty minutes after closing the door on my final client of the day, I was always struck by a ravenous need for the macaroni and cheese we kept stocked in bulk next to boxes of Small, Medium, and Large latex gloves. I would shovel food into my face like a teenage athlete and still continue to lose weight. I was in it for the excellent money, but I had never before experienced such a concentrated dose of the human condition.

Usually I spent the night between shifts with friends in Oakland but this particular Friday I had a very late client and another one scheduled for first thing the following morning. I figured it would just be easier to sleep on the bed in the Executive Dungeon.

By this point, the Big House felt like my second home. Sage encouraged us to greet arriving clients the way a hostess would treat distinguished guests. When I showed up for my shift I would stash my bike in the basement and immediately tear off all my clothes, my sweatshirt, cotton leggings, sneakers, men's boxer briefs, sports bra, band t-shirt. In fact I was quite notorious among the ladies for conducting my "behind the scenes" affairs - vacuuming, organizing the datebook, counting my money, doing paperwork - in the buff.

The Gates gave me permission to toss out any shame or confusion I had about my body and feel like a sexy woman who had no need for social niceties like clothing. Subsequently I have rented other dungeon studios where the owners are shocked by my immodesty. More than once it has been necessary for me to sheepishly explain that dungeons and nudity have become synonymous in my mind.

It was in this relaxed and naked state that I locked the door behind the last ladies working late on the Friday night shift and settled into the Executive bed. I am quite proud of my ability to make a home anywhere I lay my head and I never considered that the Big House would be any different.

That night I discovered that the wrought iron bondage bed was not made for sleeping.

Maybe stagehands have similar experiences if they get caught working late at the theater and must spend the night in a prop couch on a stage. In my dreams, every scene that had ever taken place in that room was happening at once. All night I tossed and turned as if I were trying to sleep in the middle of a kinky symphonic light show. Surreal moments of nipples extending and rods raising welts flashed through my mind. All sort of obscenities were barked over each other as if the volume of every booth at a porn shop were turned up at once.

These ghosts of the Gates were not nightmarish per se. They were just dreams that were meant for waking life, not for quotidian human functions like resting. The house Sage built had spawned a million spontaneous stories, and those stories, once given a life of their own, had entered my subconscious. They were more powerful than either the men or women who'd first conjured them during working hours; now, without the other women to protect me, I was defenseless against them.

I never slept there again and I recommended that other girls refrain from doing so as well. I had a new reverence for the power of the place.

Sage doesn't take sessions anymore. In fact, she stopped around the time I started. I was fortunate enough to see her in action once or twice when someone wanted a walk-on and no other lady was around. On one such occasion, I dashed out of the session bathroom down the stairs to find Sage drinking an afternoon beer in her office.

"I need someone for a golden shower walk on in five!"

Sage looked at the books and shrugged. "Well, I guess it's gonna have to be me."

"Is that ok?"

"Sure thing, Mistress. I'll see you up there," she said, tipping the rest of the beer down her throat.

In a few minutes, just as I was finishing pissing, there was a knock on the door. My client—lying in the bathtub as all toilet-training subs did—spluttered, "Come in!"

Sage entered the tiny bathroom. She was wearing a transparent blue teddy and no makeup, her blonde-red hair and sun-tanned skin radiating beauty.

"Well, look at this boy," she cooed. "It looks like he hasn't quite been doused enough."

Moving gracefully, like a barefoot ballerina, she mounted the lip of the tub and released a steady stream of hot piss all over the client, who may not have even realized how lucky he was.

Bianca Stone

h a i r

Bianca Stone

Bianca Stone is 5'9 in flats, wiry and muscular **with legs for days.** She moves with a liquid purpose. **She is stunning** in comfortable clothes without makeup; **and in maroon lipstick, black eyeliner,** heels and lingerie she is a mean-looking, **head-turning fox.**

Her hair, which serves as both her political and artistic expression, is thick and dark brown. It grows freely on her legs, under her arms, and over her crotch, with the soft matted quality of hair that hasn't been close to a razor for years.

In addition to mixing cocktails at a bar in her North Oakland neighborhood, the twenty-four year old Bianca makes a living performing sex in films, on live cam, and onstage. She is also a full-service sexual provider for private clients.

Bianca never really fit into the "natural hippie girl" look that is generally associated with what little hairiness can be found in porn being produced today. She describes herself as a "surly queer bitch," and she has never had much success attempting to dial that down. Her body is covered in tattoos of obscure mystic symbols. She is a politically radical student, an intellectual performance artist.

Many people see women with body hair as unclean, and assume they will smell bad. Body hair is also seen as a demarcation of lesbianism, much as fastidious grooming is a stereotype associated with gay men.

In reality, of course, there are many reasons to be hairy. A general inquiry of my unshaven female friends reveals reasons that range from a calculated political statement, to aesthetic or sensual preference, to plain laziness.

Though we did not meet each other there, Bianca and I

both spent a few formative years of our early twenties in a central California coastal town called Santa Cruz.

The University of California Santa Cruz campus is located in the redwood forest at the base of the Santa Cruz Mountains. The town's beaches combine the Southern California stereotype of surfing and roller coasters with the quieter foggy cliff sides of the state's northern coasts. Many hippies-cum-yuppies have settled there and the commerce caters to their lifestyle; everywhere you look you'll find black light posters of Hendrix, Marley, and Joplin, vegan food, and sustainable clothing. Drifters of all ages pass through and some never leave. Suburban kids who are slumming it as anarchists blend in with those who are actually destitute. Radical politics prevail, even if people are just trying it on for size.

It's therefore rare to see young women with makeup and trendy clothes on the streets of this town. Comfort is highly valued. While it is generally warm all year round, the coastline can bring in a foggy chill. Everyone—men, women, kids, rich, broke—wears hoodie sweatshirts. Conventional capitalism is also frowned upon so clothes that are clearly secondhand are prized over clothes that are obviously stylish.

As for grooming, men tend to wear beards. On women, hairy legs and armpits are not necessarily a codified signal of being gay, or even of being an outspoken feminist. It's simply accepted and encouraged to be relaxed.

When Bianca moved to Santa Cruz from the suburban mid-West, she was thrilled to participate in progressive social conversations. She asked herself many questions she had always taken for granted: To what degree do class standards of hygiene unnecessarily deplete resources? How much bathing is actually required to be clean? Is cleanliness defined as freedom from disease? What indicates an unclean person? Can people recognize the difference in smell between a body that is breeding harmful bacteria and a body that just doesn't smell like a product from the shopping mall?

In fact, it was so commonplace to not shave in Santa Cruz that Bianca didn't have much a political context for her choice. "It wasn't until I came to the Bay Area, which is a big metropolitan city with more of a variety of gender aesthetics happening for female-bodied people, that I started to contextualize a more political identity behind it," she tells me.

By the time she made that move, she had already been doing sex work in Santa Cruz for two years. Shortly after moving to California, Bianca had begun selling her panties online.

Marketing herself as a hairy Jewish American Princess, she bought packs of white underwear and sold them on *EBanned.net*, an auction site that allows the adult-themed items that E Bay does not.

Bianca admired her panty-buying clients. Many of them couldn't afford $300 an hour for a full-service provider, but still wanted to feel a more tactile human connection than porn provides. She saw it as a sort of sex work pen-palling or ritual magic. She would write a letter on her typewriter and enclose some sort of extra small token in each package.

This character she created—the spoiled rich girl whose Daddy had cut her off, who "didn't want to get a real job"—proved very successful. Bianca started making $20-60 per panty. Clearly there was something about helping a gorgeous brat maintain her relaxed lifestyle that some men found arousing.

Ironically enough, this period was the first time Bianca had been financially independent her entire life.

Bianca grew up in Dearborne, Illinois, a wealthy white North-Shore suburb of Chicago. Her father is a second-generation American whose grandmother emigrated from Russia. Her mother is Lebanese and Columbian.

She had a very comfortable childhood. Her father, who was successful in the diamond retail business, did not raise Bianca to be financially self-sufficient (although he did give her brother that guidance). Instead, at the age of thirteen, she was—in her words—"given to the gym," and began training to be a rhythmic Olympic athlete. She traveled the world by herself.

The first time she ever visited California and developed crushes on the gym girls she met there, she knew she wanted to return to live among the "freaky gay people."

Due to her gymnastics career, Bianca actually

started shaving earlier than most girls. While today clients love her hair because it is a sign of her maturity, many of her female peers in middle school were envious of the fact that Bianca was allowed to shave. They associated hair with their own adolescence and smooth female bodies with adulthood.

A few years into high school she sustained a major injury and was forced to wear a back brace, making her an outcast. Her pain meds became her new social capital, and she began "running with the fast crowd." During this time, she experienced a great deal of traumatic slut-shaming and sexual abuse.

This era is what she considers her earliest practice for sex work. She would flirt with men for booze, drugs, and access to clubs. By the time the prospect of actually doing it for money appeared on her radar, it came naturally to her. In fact, connecting with men online first instead of meeting them on the street felt significantly safer.

Bianca came out as queer on her birthright trip to Israel. She was eighteen and had just graduated from high school. As a queer femme, she found the Chicago scene to be a boys club of bathhouses and gay bars. "I still had the fantasy that California radicals would be the ones to turn me out," she says.

So Bianca moved to Santa Cruz for school. Soon after, her dad went bankrupt and had a nervous breakdown. She knew she was financially draining him so she decided it was time to take care of herself.

"I don't identify as someone who does survival

sex work no matter how broke I am, because there's always a home and food for me in Chicago. As long as they don't know I'm a sex worker, they'll take me in."

Bianca joined a growing number of unshaven women who modeled for Hairy Girl niche porn companies, doing strip tease photo sets and masturbation videos. Eventually she graduated to hardcore girl-on-girl scenes and live online cam shows. She decided to start escorting when a fellow hairy girl recommended a client; it felt like a natural transition. Soon after, she moved north to Oakland in search of more queer sex worker community and higher paying clients.

The Bay Area is not only a hub for international business; daily commuters drive and ride trains in from towns from hundreds of miles away. For people who want to hire an escort far from their daily life, their workday gives them plenty of opportunities.

Bianca was ambitious and ingenious. She knew she had to come up with a strategy to stand out from the saturated escort market. Every quality that made her appealing to prospective clients was offset by her tattoos and unwillingness to conform to someone else's expectations of how she should behave sexually. So she decided to market herself as an unshaven escort, a Hairy Girl you could spend an hour or two with.

Her subsequent experience was not an uncommon one for those in the sex industry who represent something unconventional. The clients who did find her were searching through thousands of pictures for the one rare thing they wanted; in this case, a beautiful woman who didn't shave. These clients, although relatively fewer, tend to be more devoted and reverent because what they desire is that much more difficult to find.

"On my escort ad," Bianca explains, "I link the idea of my body hair to the promotion of natural wellness that's really popular these days. I'm using that and marketing that. I don't use any chemical cosmetics or fragrances. There's some people who have allergies to fragrances, so I'm a chemical-scent-free escort, which is interesting because there's not a lot of that. And I write on my ads; 'so you can enjoy all my natural smells.' A lot of people, not just those who like a top bush but full wild untouched body hair, they *do* like my smells. A really popular sex act in my sessions is to let them eat my armpits out. They love to be smothered with my hairy armpits in their face. It's like sex for them. And they love the smell. I stopped wearing deodorant to my sessions. We live in this overly hygienic world. We've lost our sense of the smell of other bodies. Smells seem dirty and gross—we forget how sexually arousing that can be and we don't have that in our realm anymore. Some people are searching for that and the body hair is a way to indicate it."

In the sex industry, characteristics of the female body are seen as codes for a style of satisfaction. A woman covered in tattoos, for example, is seen as tough and dominant. Blondes are submissive sex kittens, brunettes are the girls next door, and redheads are a bit wild. The reductiveness of perceived race is especially problematic. Asian women must decide if they are going to be the corruptible schoolgirl or the ruthless goddess. Black women must face assumptions about their insatiability; Latin women, their wild temperaments. Mixed-race women must decide if they want to pass as white or play up their "exotic" qualities.

Bianca's Ashkenazi Jewish, Latin, and Arabic heritage makes it possible for her to market herself as a light-skinned woman of color or a very tanned white woman. She has the privilege of a very pretty face and a naturally slender body, making her attractive to a broad range of clients. Thus she describes her choice to identify as a Hairy Girl as an act of solidarity with the people who work in the sex industry who cannot change the qualities that marginalize them.

As for the kind of clients Bianca and her niche characteristics attract, it's simply a matter of taste. Many middle-aged or older clients are nostalgic for a time when shaving was not the norm. Bianca has some clients who tell her that being with unshaven girls reminds them of their college girlfriends. She also postulates that some clients look for hairy girls to assuage their guilt at the infantilized images of women that dominate our culture. Then there are the people who love to be smothered in natural, chemical-free scents. Choosing Bianca is like choosing a sustainably-made sweater or an organic banana.

Bianca leads with her values. She speaks often of personal growth, of creative inspiration, of politics, of community. For her, being an anti-establishment whore doesn't just mean she has an edgy look. It means being conscious of her radical politics while she works: being aware of money and how it moves through her labor, being humane to her clients, and using her free time for art and activism.

By the time I started domming at the age of twenty-four, being hairy was so much a part of my identity that it actually never occurred to me to shave my legs, armpits, or crotch as part of my new professional sex kitten routine.

As it turned out, my assumption that I could do great business as a Bay Area sex worker without making this particular concession to conventional femininity proved to be correct. Working in a house with other ladies was like finishing school in many ways. I learned how to attach garter belts to silk stockings, how to walk in six-inch stilettos. For a while I wrote this off as drag, until I realized it was the contrast between my glamorous persona and my more androgynous body that made me feel powerful and excited. I represented myself on my own terms, picking and choosing gender signifiers.

I would go into sessions in bright red pumps, a

black lace thong, glossy lips, pink eye-shadow, my nails painted purple, with transparent silk stockings pressing down the fine soft light brown hair on my legs. The slightly darker, wiry hair under my arms peeked out from the frame of my push-up bra. A boyfriend had introduced me to the sensual fun of shaving my pubic hair, so my bush fluctuated in size and shape.

I can only recall one time that a client booked with me and then, upon sitting in the negotiation room and getting an eyeful of my body hair, opted to walk. "I just can't get into it," he said, handing me the house's requisite $20 walking fee. More often, if clients spoke of it at all, it was so say, "I never thought I would like leg hair, but because it's on you, and I like you, now I like it." Or, charmingly, "It's not your hair I'm lookin' at, honey."

I didn't make an effort to hide my body hair in my promotional pictures but I also never specifically mentioned, eroticized, or emphasized it.

Bianca Stone emphasizes it.

In her portfolio pictures, she's lifting her elbow and running her fingers through her underarm hair. On her Twitter and Tumblr, she is always spinning new fetish terms like "femme bear", and bragging about her "full fur."

In marketing her body and sexuality, she has taken a part of herself that she doesn't want to change, and commodified it. She has transformed this quality into the reason you *should* hire her rather than the reason you might choose another, more conventional playmate.

October 2012: Bianca has flown to New York City to shoot content for a new project she's developing and I've told her she can stay with me. She flies in late at night so I leave the door unlocked. When I wake in the morning, there she is on a mat on the floor, a tangle of limbs and dark frizzy hair. I start making coffee and she croaks my name in a husky smoker's voice.

Fetish photographer Bob Coulter is picking her up at noon, so she starts putting her outfit together. Friends have lent her pieces of fur and scraps of leather, which she uses to throw together a costume meant to evoke Tina Turner in *Beyond Thunderdome*. The only accessory she requires for her bottom half is her magnificent bush.

The whole time she is getting ready, she is manic, chatty, and breathless. She seems to have a lot to prove, having just quit drinking; it's as if she contains an excess of neurotic energy that she has been dousing for years. She throws baby powder on her head and explains to me—twice—that this is called whore shampoo because it quickly returns volume to dirty hair.

On a walk to the corner drug store for maroon-colored cock-sucking lipstick (i.e. lipstick that stays on all day), she wears her leopard print platform shoes. She is now over six feet tall and doesn't seem remotely concerned with being conspicuous.

Bob arrives; air-kissing me, Bianca dashes out the door. My ears are almost ringing from her presence and it makes me think of the manic energy that sex work used to give me. I too used to rush from planes to people's couches to photo shoots to clients: applying liquid eyeliner on a moving train, grabbing enema bottles on my way to a hotel. These days, I take several hours to settle into my persona and, later, to decompress out of the state induced by being that person.

I turn back to my desk and my coffee.

Later Bianca will send me prints of this photoshoot in the mail. There is one that depicts her on train tracks pretending to eat road kill. She looks vicious and primal, yet somehow not predatory. She is always smiling, relishing her exhibitionism. In another she spreads her legs on a cheap Jersey motel bed. Brightly colored cartoons on the television in the background contrast with the bright white of a tank top tied around her small breasts. She is throwing back her head in eye-squeezing, grinning ecstasy, slipping her finger through a rainbow-sprinkled doughnut and into her crotch.

This is the print I put above my desk.

⸮

The next day, Bianca and I walk up Ninth Avenue to my friend's apartment. He has offered the use of his place for the weekend, provided I water his plants and feed his cat, Ozone. It's a two-bedroom walk-up with plain white walls and a skylight—perfect for shooting amateur porn.

This is all part of the next stage of Bianca's plan to change the way hairy women are perceived in the collective sexual imagination: a website called *Hairy Kink*. Most commercial sexual media that depicts girls with body hair is made by men and sticks to a very strict idea of what a Hairy Girl is like: a sweet, natural girl next door, an ideal girlfriend, an innocent teenager just discovering her body. Bianca wants to change all that by producing content that is nasty and taboo.

Bella Vendetta and her friend Bev arrive. Bella is curvaceous and stunning, with pale white skin and jet black hair. Heavily tattooed and interested in extreme kinks like knives and hook suspensions, she is a relaxed, naturally dominant character. There's little difference between the woman you see leering from her website and the woman who walks into our temporary little studio. Bella isn't as scary in person as one might expect, but every bit as formidable a presence.

By contrast, this is one of Bianca's first times actually running a production. She is stressed about her new camera. She wants to make a shoot list. Basically she wants to do so many of the things she thinks she should do that she doesn't end up doing any of the basic things she needs to do. She wants to shoot a soft-core scene; a scene in which Bella and I dominate her; a pantyhose fetish scene; a fisting scene; a photoset; a Behind the Scenes interview. She'll pay $50, she'll pay $200, she forgot to print the 2257 and model release forms. When she asks my advice I give it to her, but mostly I trust her to figure it all out herself. I like to run a tight ship on my sets, but this is not my set.

Bev is making a documentary about Bella, so she has agreed to shoot the hardcore footage today. This kind of trade economy has become more prevalent among indie porn during the recession. Bella and Bianca will get footage for their site, Bev will get footage for her doc, and I'm getting my story.

Bella and I are both working pro-dommes, so growing out our body hair has been an act of solidarity with Bianca's vision for her project. It's simple enough to say to a client, "I'm growing out my hair for a hairy kink porn shoot, isn't that exotic?" or in Bella's case, probably something more along the lines of; "Mistress does what she wants, bitch."

However, the client may ultimately choose to see someone else who is consistently shaven. So it's a gamble.

"You guys have such epic bushes! I've been growing mine out for two months and it's nothing like yours," Bella moans, peering over her leather corset to her crotch.

Bubbling over with ideas, Bianca is having trouble deciding what to do when: she wants to do a solo masturbation scene; she wants to spank and beat me.

It's Bella, in her natural sternness, who says "Well, I think that we have about four hours, so you do the solo scene, and then we'll dominate you. Sound good?" This last question is for my benefit.

"Oh, yeah, don't look at me. I'm just a pretty face," I say, sipping my coffee.

Bianca's momentum falters, almost tripping over Bella's clarity. I see her generate a protest, think better of it, and swallow it in a wave of thought. Instead, she draws herself up, composing herself as director/top.

"Alright!" she chirps.

She explains to Bev what she wants from the masturbation scene: the camera will act as a POV character coming in from the hall, moving slowly across the living room, and tentatively opening the door to the bedroom. There, Bianca will be sprawled out naked, as if she has passed out after a night of partying. She indicates all this with huge sweeping motions of her hands and you can see the gymnast choreographer in her. You can also tell she is very nervous from the way she repeats every detail of the blocking several times.

I have to remind her at least twice when she opens the door not to speak loudly about porn in the hallway where the neighbors might hear and to make certain the front door closes behind her so Ozone doesn't dash out.

Once the camera starts rolling, once Bev stalks through the living room and "discovers" Bianca in bed, something switches. Bella and I sit on the living room couch and stare into space as if we are listening to a radio program, occasionally turning and giving each other smirks when Bianca does or says something that pleases us.

Bianca is in character, and the pressure in the room changes with the thick heavy syrup of her talent and sex appeal.

"Whhaaat are you doing here?" she asks the future voyeurs, the potential customers, the masturbating fans who are implied beyond the camera lens.

Now, if I were doing a scene where I was acting out a fantasy of being discovered, I would probably put on what I like to call my Laura Palmer voice, a pitch higher and an implied several dozen IQ points lower than my normal register. It's a voice with a campy breathiness, a voice that comes from my head instead of my diaphragm, a voice accompanied by saucer eyes, a voice that is just over the top enough to convince the person for whom it is the benefit that this is really, really happening to them.

Bianca, on the other hand uses her real voice, and it has a very convincing quality of having been caught unawares. She begins, seductively, to strip off her panties.

"Did you know under my clothes that I have a hairy pussy? Do you like it?"

There is so much suggested by the little narration Bianca is improvising. There is the hint of sleep rape, as if the viewer is someone who is trying to justify taking advantage of a passed out drunk girl. It also possibly contains something cathartic for Bianca, who has very recently left her partying days behind her. There's the invasion of a woman's space, and the paradoxical fantasy that she might get off on sharing her privacy. There's the tease and denial, the orgasm control, the casual control of the voyeur that is much more real life bitchy girl than supreme dominatrix.

Bianca seems to be essentially talking dirty to herself, working herself up, putting on a show for her own benefit. Bella and I can hear in her voice how she's getting more and more aroused as she masturbates.

Bianca is essentially freestyling on a theme, narrating what happens to her brain when she becomes aroused. This may be a fantasy she has in common with her clients, or she may just have this routine down.

"I love being watched when I touch my hairy pussy," she groans.

Presently, we hear an orgasm, and it's difficult to tell whether she's faking it or not. She recovers quickly and then addresses the camera as if she had forgotten, in her horniness, that it was watching her.

"Well! I got what I wanted! Now get out of here before I call my boyfriend! Go on! Get out!"

Bev backs awkwardly out of the room, then turns and pretends to hurry out the door.

There is a beat, and then we explode into applause.

Bianca emerges from the room in euphoria,

that particular sex work union of post orgasmic and post-performance.

In the next shoot, Bianca wants us to get into the fetish possibilities of hair. She wants hair bondage and hair pain. She wants hair to be both a possibility for humiliation and for power.

"Do *you* actually like your body hair?" I ask her, suddenly curious.

Bianca grins. "I will say, sometimes when I get nervous I reach into my underarms and play with my armpit hair." She demonstrates. "Sometimes I rub my bush hair. I don't know why, I don't know how to articulate it, but sometimes stroking my body hair grounds me and makes me feel calm. I don't know where that comes from. But I like the sensation. I like feeling furry. It makes me feel more like an animal, which is very grounding to me."

So Bella and I use her underarm hair for bondage. We pull on it to make her squeal with pain. We use it as intimidation, degradation, and praise.

Ozone frequently wanders into the scene looking completely uninterested but leaving huge piles of cat hair to remind us of his presence.

Lying in a beaten fucked puddle on the hardwood floor, Bianca is grinning like a maniac. She's getting the content she wants, she's making the statement she wants. She's an anti-capitalist entrepreneur.

♩

When I moved to New York City in 2011, I was convinced that Bianca Stone was going to be the next big hotshot loud-mouthed sex worker that ruled the Bay Area. She was about five years younger than me, unabashedly anarchic, and she just oozed wild sex appeal. Writing this story about her made me feel a continued connected to the dangerous vitality of sex work even though I was inching towards retirement.

Then Bianca disappeared.

The last time I saw her was my thirtieth birthday in 2012, when I was visiting Oakland. She picked me up, drove me to the grocery store and to a BBQ. We were both wearing second hand motorcycle jackets and black rompers.

She told me about a shoot she had done for *Kink.com* wherein she had allowed herself to be shaved on camera as part of the scene's humiliation. I watched the trailer later. It's brutal and hilarious. It perfectly encapsulates San Francisco BDSM porn, in that a company would allow a beautiful woman her expression of iconoclasm under the condition that it be used against her in a torture scenario.

I asked Bianca how she felt about being shaven, when she had worked so hard to build her brand as a hairy model.

"Whatever," she shrugged. "It grows back."

Bianca sat on a panel I moderated at that year's Feminist Porn Conference, telling an audience of hundreds of people that her family had excommunicated her when she told them she was supporting herself with escorting and porn. She wore a purple galaxy print jumpsuit all weekend and started at least one Twitter war.

Some time after that, I started to notice her Tumblr, Facebook, and Twitter had been deactivated: the 21st century version of ceasing to exist. When I started asking around, nobody really understood why she stopped being a star or where she had gone. Several people told me she had moved to the woods to practice witchcraft, which is frankly not as far-fetched as you might think.

It turned out that Bianca was in fact the raw, pulsating id of the sex worker rights movement. She passionately used her body as a brazen example of her politics; but she wasn't stable and she couldn't sustain it.

Bianca's close friend, Nikki Silver, who has managed to make a sustainable business out of being a hairy girl with her site *Naughty Natural,* told me she is pretty sure Bianca just wants to be left alone:

> *She found solace from the limelight that she had conflicted feelings about in the queer/trans woodsy witch community and maybe needed to take a big step back from the public eye to recover from throwing herself into it.*

In a way, Bianca isn't really Bianca any more. Her sex work persona was a flaming costume, destined to be all volume and flash. When it burned out, she was left as whoever she was on the inside all along. So she retreated to the woods, to howl at the moon.

Nigel Matthews

desire

Nigel Matthews

When I was a kid, I fantasized constantly about **being kidnapped.** Inspired by the true-life **horror story of** Polly Klaus and fictionalized **serial killer scenarios** like those of *The Silence of the Lambs,* **I imagined** that I was completely vulnerable to the will of men with terrible, terrible intentions.

I wasn't a particularly overprotected child, but somehow the media led me to believe that I could be snatched up at any time, even from the apparent safety of my bunk bed.

I would be smuggled away and placed in some horrible basement, subjected to unimaginable humiliation and torture. BUT! I would be so cunning, so industrious, so courageous, so much more of a match for these kidnappers than my innocent looks belied, that I would withstand everything they could dish out and eventually escape.

The entire world would be searching in vain to rescue me, but I would rescue myself! No rope could bind me. No gag could quiet me. There was nothing I couldn't endure without my spirit fully intact. Wearing a filthy white slip, I would bravely walk barefoot, find the authorities, lead them to the hideout, identify my assailants, and get my face plastered across every newspaper in the world as the smartest, boldest little bitch in America!

When I grew up, I got to be that little kidnapped heroine for a living. As a professional submissive, I escaped and triumphed over and over again.

My willingness to play that role was how I got to meet people like Nigel Matthews.

Nigel likes to play rough with bondage, hair-pulling, and face-slapping. He loves to admire ladies in delicate, lacy lingerie and kitten heels, silk stockings and garter belts. But more than all of these things, Nigel's passion is for spanking women.

To call Nigel a spanker is sort of like calling Baryshnikov a dancer or Coltrane a saxophonist. As a spanking top playing a fantasy scene, he is precise, alert, innovative, intuitive, subtle, and passionate.

I can say this with confidence because he has been hiring me for spanking sessions for over five years.

Nigel is always threatening to write down his story, but he can't seem to find the time. I asked if he would let me interview him for posterity and he enthusiastically agreed. We met in a five-star hotel in a New England city. The room in which the interview was conducted resembled any one of dozens of such rooms we had played in over the years. The starched white sheets, the little bottles of complimentary lotion, the empty room service trays were all interchangeable in our shared memories.

It's not just Nigel's English accent that makes his voice so seductive. Like him, it is calm and elegantly masculine. He thinks everything through before putting it to words. There is an almost religious awe in his voice when he speaks of his spanking art and about the women he's played with. His stories have the well-rehearsed quality of a man who has been telling them to himself in his head for years before he ever got the chance to speak them aloud. His demeanor while telling them has the quality of someone who is deeply grateful for the chance to share a passion he might have otherwise have had to keep pent up inside.

Nigel was born in Southern England on the outskirts of London in 1962. He moved to America in the mid-80's for a job and has lived on the East Coast ever since.

Although he remembers his parents using corporal punishment on his brothers (who, he points out, weren't worse behaved than he was—just worse about getting caught) and the headmaster at his all-boy's boarding school using a cane, he does not attribute his proclivities to these early experiences.

Nevertheless, Nigel has had spanking on the brain since he was about eleven or twelve years old. He describes his earliest fantasies:

> *It was always about me being seated, fully clothed and pulling a girl or a woman across my lap and spanking her on the seat of her skirt. She'd always be wearing a skirt or dress. Then pulling that up and seeing her panties and spanking her on her panty bottom and then pulling them down. I think my fantasies mostly centered on girls or women who wanted to be spanked. They might play at struggling but they weren't really trying to get away. But then I'd have some fantasies where it was a punishment, where I was holding or pinning the person down and they might be crying out. I had both kinds.*

He was also much more fixated on women's derrieres, on their "flaring of hips from waist," than on breasts, as most of his male friends seemed to be.

By the time he was a teenager, Nigel was getting his hands on the spanking magazines that were very popular in England such as *Janus, Pheonix, Kane*. In his thirties he discovered videos and novels by a company called Shadow Lane, whose tagline is,"The Romance of Spanking." Nigel developed a taste for the techniques in these videos and especially the fact that the female performers seemed to be actually enjoying their punishment.

He had always imagined that if he could ever spank someone, it would be because she agreed to *endure* it. The idea of a real live woman wanting to receive it as much as he wanted to give it had hardly crossed his mind.

He attempted to spank his early sexual partners and "was always rebuffed." So he led what he describes as a normal vanilla sex life. Yet thoughts of spanking persisted, remaining a secret obsession. For twenty-five years, this obsession consumed his private inner life, his pornography collection, and his masturbation routines.

Until he decided to do something about it.

🌶

On October 27th 2007, Nigel came to see me at the

Gates for the first time. He was forty-nine, and I was twenty-five. He had been spanking professionals like myself for over five years at this point, but I knew none of this for quite some time. All he knew about me was the persona I spun in my ads. My particular shape was clearly a key attraction but he says it was my description of myself on my ads that really drew him in.

I can vividly recall the moment I opened the door and welcomed this man into the house's negotiation room. He loomed over me at 6'2", slender and well mannered with soft silver hair. His grey suit was well fitting and clean, his hands recently manicured. His eyes were large and blue; capable, even in that first moment, of enormous intensity.

I had been a sex worker for about a year and was just starting to settle into thinking I knew what the hell I was doing. I could be snappy and sassy. I was learning how to negotiate, how to maintain limits within a scene. I was learning what I could take and what I liked.

The entry in the Gate's card catalogue for that session reads as follows:

10.24.07. Nigel. British, grey-haired, handsome. Role Play: I seduced him at my birthday party. I got spanked, then Holly and Lenore got spanked. We also got belted and hairbrushed. Then we switched to a "Story of O" roleplay. I had displeased my master and he punished me

with flogger and verbal humiliation. my pussy
was dripping wet. no self release. very respectful.
stuck to negotiation. best impact play of my life.

Everyone at the Gates was required to "switch,"
which means they both took sessions in which they
were dominant and also sessions in which the client
was dominant and the lady was submissive. I was
developing a reputation as an exceptional pro-sub,
mostly because I always felt that this gave me more
power and control than domming did. Experiencing
physical pain with strictly respected limits gave me
a chance to test my endurance and feel incredibly
proud.

That said, as much as I enjoyed my job, it was still
laborious. I always relished a break from the intense
sensations the client often dished out.

Not with Nigel.

When Nigel gave me a break, I found myself feeling like a greedy petulant child.

I found myself wanting to be spanked *some more.*

That session was something entirely new to me.
While remaining within the limits of our professional
boundaries and our negotiated scene, I was able to
learn new things about my own desires.

When Nigel turned forty, two tragedies pushed him

to finally pursue the realization of his lifelong desire: the shock of September 11th, and the loss of a close friend to a terminal illness. The Internet made it possible for him to find a place called The Chateau in Los Angeles.

I had no idea at all that a place like that existed. And here it was, quite clearly a dungeon, with multiple ladies working out of it, most of them in a dom role, some switches, one or two submissive. In fact there might have only been three or four ladies on that site but I very quickly fastened on one of them. Her name was Clare, and there were probably just two photos of her there. She was in a short plaid skirt and white panties and she looked delectable. She had a round bottom, a cherubic face and she looked saucy. I knew I wanted to spank her.

Despite some reservations, Nigel figured that his first spanking needed to be with a professional. Though he'd been to a few strip clubs, his lack of confidence had kept him from enjoying himself. Somehow he'd become convinced that sex work must be connected to organized crime, and that he would be blackmailed if he tried to hire someone to fulfill his obsession.

But he had made up his mind to overcome his shame and paranoia, determined that this was something he needed to experience. He rearranged a West

Coast business trip so he could get to L.A. to see Clare. He called and booked an hour session, which cost $120. He was so eager not to be late that he arrived three hours early for his appointment.

It was in an industrial back area of North Holly-wood on a dead-end road and I saw this little brick building on the left with a red light and 'Chateau' over the window. . . . I drove to the end of the road and turned around and parked. It was dark. I remember sitting there thinking, 'You don't have to do this. You could just drive away now and nothing would happen. You wouldn't be making a mistake.' And then I thought, 'But if I get out of the car, I'm doing it.' I sat there for about another minute, turned the engine off and got out.

I walked across the street, and opened the door, and there was sort of an entry area the size of a hotel room. There was a desk counter in front of the door and there was a guy sitting there. He was probably about seventy, smoking. And behind him was a peg board and on that peg board was just about every spanking implement that I had ever seen. And ropes and cuffs and chains and gags. I looked at that wall and thought, 'This is the place.'

I walked up to the guy, and I said 'My name's Nigel, I've got an appointment.' He looked at his book and I said, 'Yeah, the appointment isn't until 11 o clock.' The guy looked at me funny and he looked down at the book and then hit an intercom and said, 'Clare! Your 11 o clock's early!' I just remember being so embarrassed. I was thinking, 'This isn't good.' And then I was thinking, 'This is so, so good!'

There was a dark curtain there, and it got pulled aside and Claire came out. She looked every bit her picture except taller because of course she was in three-inch heels. I introduced myself and she said, "Come back here, we need to talk." We went into one of the dungeon rooms, and of course it had a spanking bench and a St. Andrew's cross and I was gawking at things. She sat me down and sat opposite. She had really long legs and of course all her thighs were showing, the skirt she was wearing was tiny. I remember I started to sweat and she said, 'So, tell me what you're here for.'

And I said, 'I want to spank you.' And then I just gushed my life story. I told her I'd always been into spanking, it's been a life-long fantasy, I'd never done it, I really wanted to spank her, I wanted to do a role-play, I had a role-play in mind.

She kind of reached across and patted me on the wrist and said, "It's gonna be ok."

The role-play was: a longtime platonic friend, someone who I had always fancied but had never been interested in me, had broken up with her boyfriend. She then confesses to me that *she had actually always really liked me but had this fetish that she was too embarrassed to tell me about. And then she tells me about it and of course, we learn about it together. . . .*

So we finished negotiation, and she said, 'Well, we should go get some toys!' And I said, 'Really? I thought for my first time, it would just be a hand spanking. . . .' And she said 'Nonsense! We need toys! You'll want to try them. I know you will.' She marched me back out front, and we went through the peg board and picked out four or five. We used all of them, a leather paddle, a little leather slapper, a strap, a riding crop, and - and this one just blew my mind that she picked it up - a cane. So the very first time that I spanked somebody I got to cane her as well. But only a few little love pats. I was always afraid of the cane and until I learned how to use it, I didn't use it very hard.

I felt like I'd won the lottery. We sat next to each other on a bench or a couch and we played out our role-play and then of course it came to the point where she needed to go across my lap. I remember putting my left hand on her forearm and my right hand on her shoulder and guiding her across my lap; that wonderful warm heavy feeling of a woman draped across my lap for the first time. As soon as she was across and in place, I smoothed my hand down her back and up and over her bottom across the skirt and onto her bare

thighs and somehow that was ok. It felt beautiful.
Then I rested my hand on her bottom and started
to spank.

Very softly at first and then harder through
that pleated skirt and I just couldn't believe I
was there. I was holding her, almost hugging her
across my lap and starting to spank a real woman,
a beautiful woman, and she wanted to be spanked.
Yes, she's taken money for it but everything about
the interview and how she put me at ease and how
she described what would happen . . . she wanted
to be there. That was important. And then I of
course pulled up her skirt and started spanking
her on her panties and on the part of her bottom
that protrudes from her panties. Suddenly I'm
spanking on real skin and I'm giving her several
sharp spanks and squeezing and stroking and
then sharper spanks. Then I asked her to ask me
to take down her panties and she did and I put my
fingers into her waistband and very slowly drew
them down.

The ceremony is so important to me. The cer-
emony of starting on the skirt and then on the
panties and then drawing those panties down.
There's something very special and romantic
about a woman asking me to take her panties
down. It feels like such a power trip, and such a
giving thing. And then her bottom was bare, with
a strip of panty fabric at the top of her thighs.
Then I spanked her some more.

I know I would have spread those spanks around her cheeks. She had ample bottom cheeks so I had a palate to work with. I drew her panties all the way down and she kicked them off and spread her legs a little. Of course that meant I could see things I'd never expected to see: pussy showing between her bottom cheeks. I spanked her some more and her bottom started getting redder than pink and she made some noises but it was quite clear I wasn't hurting her. I gave her a few spanks on the tops of her thighs and she squealed. I smoothed and massaged and I knew it was time to try an implement. At that point she tapped my leg and said, "May I get up sir?" Of course she'd been over my lap for some time and the blood had gone to her head. In those days I wasn't thinking of that. I do now. I get a submissive up every few minutes so that doesn't happen. But there was a glorious first ten minutes. It took me into a whole new realm of my life.

⚰

I have more than a few self-aggrandizing clients who brag to me about how much pro-subs love playing with them, that I am really in for a treat, that they're "not like other guys." More often than not, this is an indication that the opposite is actually true. Nigel is not a braggart; his clean friendly demeanor and excellent skills speak for themselves. At many houses his outstanding reputation as a client precedes him.

Still, if he had told me the Clare story before I had met and played with him, I would have assumed that she was just doing her job. But when he says that he can tell when a woman is really enjoying herself, I believe him. I've experienced it first hand, and you have to get up pretty early in the morning to fool a dominatrix.

I treasure my professional relationship with Nigel and I value him as a friend. Our relationship is characterized by a mutual openness of spirit, of gameness, of being patient, of being compassionate, of rolling with the punches. It's characterized by contrasts—by dark fantasy and sensible reality, by the enacting of ruthless brutality followed by the application of tender care, by loyalty despite distance. We provide emotional support for one another and of course have a great deal of fun together.

What really sets Nigel apart is that he is very romantic without assuming he can transgress professional boundaries. He really does eroticize limits. The same qualities that make him a successful engineer predispose him to be an excellent top. I think as an engineer he is in love with design. He pays meticulous attention to detail in what he can control while accepting and enjoying what he must leave up to chance.

One of the things I've learned over the years is, I

get the biggest thrill out of her pleasure. When I turn somebody on through spanking or punishment or role-play or voice . . . When I see and feel that effect, that's what gives me the biggest thrill. And yeah, I love the percussion, and the sting in my hand and the ritual and seeing her bottom go pink and then red. If I'm using the cane, seeing those parallel stripes come into place. But it's nothing compared to feeling that shudder or hearing that sigh or squeal and knowing that's pleasure, especially when you sense that it's unexpected pleasure. That's my biggest thrill.

I know several pro-dommes who don't do submissive scenes with anyone other than Nigel, because his sessions are such a pleasure. The way he holds a power dynamic and generates trust is extraordinary. You can surrender and give yourself over to him.

[There is] a game I like to play with a spankee the first time I see her in a professional environment. That is, after we've done our role-play and I've warmed her up and hand spanked her and perhaps used an implement or two and things are going well. We'll take a little break and then I'll put her back over my lap. I'll pull one of her hands into the small of her back and I'll hold it and tell her we're going to play a game. I'm gonna start spanking her very, very softly, and if she squeezes my hand I'll spank a little harder and the harder she

squeezes the harder I'll spank. If she releases the
pressure I'll slow down. If she releases complete-
ly I'll stop. I've probably played that game with
thirty different women and every one of them has
tried to see how much she could take! They'll ex-
periment a little bit, they'll squeeze, they'll let go,
they'll squeeze harder and hold and let go. Then
every time they squeeze they squeeze harder and
hold longer. Some of them will start squealing and
kicking and they won't let go ... until they do. I
don't believe anyone does that unless they're hav-
ing fun. I have a lot of fun with that game, too,
although sometimes it really hurts my hand!

ﻉ

Ten years later, in 2012, Nigel estimates that he has
spanked something close to one hundred women. He
discovered BDSM houses similar to the Chateau in
the Bay Area, New York, Toronto, and other cities he
travels to for work.

Nigel acknowledges the enormous debt he owes
to BDSM sex workers. His erotic fantasies developed
for decades without ever being realized. He was finally able to put them into real physical practice because of his access to women who offered the service
of being spanked for money. The structure of hiring a
sex worker was ideal for Nigel's personality.

There is something wonderfully empowering as a top, meeting somebody where it's all about me. [When I visit a sex worker] I feel completely free to set up a fantasy that meets my needs, my whims, what I want to do that day. You can indulge in a variety of women and you're not disappointing any of them. You're not going on a date and then not calling back. There was a fair exchange. Except I'm a sucker for going back. If I see someone and I like them, I go back.

Even though women "submit" or "bottom" to him, they often have a great deal to teach him. Eventually, he would hire two women at a time for lessons in using implements: one to teach, one to receive and give feedback. His skills have grown and his passion has not diminished.

Meeting and spanking a variety of women has taught me to really feel women's bodies and feel different people's expression of their pleasure. That has really made me hypersensitive to it. Whether it's a change in temperature of skin or goosebumps or sweat or a sigh or a breath, I hear and feel things I didn't used to. I learned an incredible amount from going to dungeons, taking instruction, and playing with a variety of women with different skills and different levels of experience. It's gotten to the point where sometimes I'm the teacher. But that's ok, I'm still learning, too.

But then, [I can] come into a relationship with somebody who wants to be sexually submissive, perhaps has always fantasized about it. [I have the] expertise to make her relax, feel comfortable, and get the glorious first experience that I was so lucky to get at the hands of an expert.

As an experienced client, Nigel is very opinionated about the politics of both sex work and BDSM. He is not "out" as kinky or as a client in his everyday life, though he tries to contribute to conversations about these subjects when they do come up. He would love to see a world in which sex work was legal and socially acceptable, in which men and women could treat sex and kink as a hobby to explore.

He is frustrated by the fact that other clients mistreat sex workers, which makes it difficult for them to trust him. When it turns out that someone he has hired clearly doesn't like being spanked, and is only going through the motions, he'll just pay the money and leave.

Maybe it's just me, but I love boundaries. I've read bulletin boards for guys who go to massage parlors and dungeons, and so much of the conversation is about how to push the limits and how to get more and how to get sex. It just disgusts me, frankly. I mean, what I enjoy is—we establish the limits, and everywhere inside that line is mine and I can play right up to that line. That is joyful. Why is it when somebody sets a line, you'd want to cross it? Go find somebody with a different line!

This capacity for transformation is one of the most extraordinary things I've discovered about sexual fantasy. Nigel exemplifies what can happen when someone immerses himself in a fantasy world and come out the other end a changed man:

> *It changed my character . . . it made me far more confident. I think as I became fulfilled, I became less fearful. I no longer had this vacuum in my life where there was this dark need that . . . that made me feel dirty or shameful. I was fulfilled and there was nothing dirty or shameful about it. I was having amazing fun, other people were having great fun with me and making money.*
>
> *The other thing that happened that was very unexpected for me was I became better sexually. I was never a good lover before I learned to spank. I was hesitant, I wasn't confident, I wasn't good at it. I didn't create many orgasms in my partners. After I learned to spank, that changed, radically. I'm now a very confident lover. And I think an awful lot of it was learning women's bodies.*
>
> *I hadn't had a lot of girlfriends or sexual*

partners, and now suddenly I had played sexu-
ally with a lot of women, different women, who
reacted differently, had different needs. And I say
sexual with lots of women, I mean played with
them when they were bare or very nearly bare,
you know, touching their bottoms and thighs. In
fact, in almost all of my sex worker encounters, it
was purely spanking, there was no sex. But that
put me in touch with women's bodies, and my
libido. And I think from acting out a dominant
role over and over again with women who were
either playing submissive or really enjoyed being
submissive, I became comfortable taking control
in bed or letting go of control in bed. It made an
enormous difference. And that's affected every
part of my character. I think my confidence is
built in every aspect of my life.

I enter the dungeon with the brisk march of insolence.
My swagger is probably a touch too modern for an
Edwardian maid but the attitude is more important
than the technicalities (insofar as Nigel is concerned
at least). Anyway I'm wearing black stiletto Jimmy
Choos and a gold halter-top dress over a leather corset, so accommodations to authenticity are already being made. Our respective roles are just dress-up for the
dynamics and activities we love to sink our teeth into.

"You wanted to see me, Sir?"

Nigel is seated on the far end of the room on the steel four-poster bed, his profile to me. He is wearing a charcoal-grey suit and dress shoes. He waits, patiently, in no rush, just long enough that I start to squirm ever so slightly.

When he stands, he moves very slowly, deliberately. He catches my gaze and holds it, striding towards me until we are standing toe to toe.

"Yes. It would seem that we have a problem."

"Oh. Oh really?" I ask as if the idea of *Me* and *Problem* in the same sentence must be some kind of joke. "Look, what is this about? I have my duties and. . . ."

"I know you have your duties. You've been doing your duties a bit too well lately if you ask me."

I scoff, "What's that supposed to mean?"

Nigel seems to loom taller over me.

How the hell does he do that? I wonder.

"There is the matter of a certain . . . corset."

Now, this is the point where I'm supposed to realize I'm totally fucked. Ordinarily in a professional scene I'm more or less going through the motions of such realizations. But something about the way Nigel is embodying this role is so real that my giggles are starting to simmer down inside me. I look up directly into his eyes and my blood runs cold.

I could swear the Nigel I know is gone.

There is only the butler. And the butler is very displeased with me.

"I . . . I don't know what you're talking about," I stammer.

"Take off your dress."

I feel real fear, not staged fear, while simultaneously knowing that I am completely safe.

"What?" I protest, steeping back. "You can't make me do that."

"Oh I certainly can young lady. Take it off."

I have perfected this move: the reluctant strip tease. I reach down and pull my dress up over my head as if getting naked in front of a man is the worst thing that could possibly happen to me. Underneath, of course, is the black leather corset, cinched tight.

Nigel stalks around me, yanking the dress back down over the "stolen" article as if preserving my modesty. "What do you have to say for yourself, young lady?"

"I . . . I can explain!"

The true explanation is that I really wanted to wear my fancy new corset in session. Nigel decided instantly that the item in question would just have to be the reason for my punishment. We concluded that I had stolen it and was trying to make away with it under my clothes.

But of course, I got caught. Somehow, I always did.

"Whu-what are you gonna *do* to me?" I blubber. "I can't lose this job, I can't! You don't understand!"

Does this seem formulaic? Well, when it comes to erotic role-play, formula is key. It's sort of like jamming on the blues: when you perform a classic turnaround there is a nod to tradition. The mind is satisfied by a confirmation of expectation. Innovation and collaboration is where *style* comes in.

The butler makes me remove the corset and explains that I have two choices: get sacked, or submit to brutal corporal punishment. This turn of the scene is crucial; it creates a semblance of consent, even if in a real scenario the consent would be coerced and therefore nullified.

Nigel loves to make you admit you deserve what's coming to you.

I cast my eyes down and murmur, "Fine."

"What was that?" he bellows.

I lift my chin sharply. "Fine! Spank me! Whip me! I don't care, just get it over with!"

Nigel grabs me by the hair and forcefully yanks me over to the queen-sized bed. He pulls me over his lap. His legs are long but I settle easily onto his thighs. He begins to stroke me from the nape of my neck down my back and across my ass. His strokes are light, as if there is a fine dust on my clothes that he is gently sweeping off.

This slow start serves the same function as a dancer stretching before a show to prevent injury. It has the same anticipatory effect as the ambient hum of an orchestra warming up before a performance. It brings us into our bodies, into the moment. The excitement is buzzing through both of us, and this calm consideration helps us both to settle. He doesn't allow his adrenaline to get the better of him and I don't tense up against the pain. I know he has the integrity to take his time and he knows I am prepared to surrender.

I have been spanked by Nigel countless times and by this point there is a quick Pavlovian response to being put across his lap. I feel so clearly that I am giving him exactly what he desires and that gives me a deep satisfaction.

Strokes become taps. He drums his fingertips lightly on the heart shaped curve at the center of my ass; not light like a tickle, light like a piano player. Then he begins to slap, his blows grazing me sideways instead of hitting me directly. He moves with a moderate tempo that subdues me. This goes on for five, ten minutes. He begins to punctuate the rhythm with harder smacks. Sometimes in a predictable pattern for me to get used to, and then something harder comes unexpected and makes me cry out but also giggle. I wail and writhe but keep position.

Ceremoniously, he pulls up my skirt.

Spanks me on my pink lacy panties for a while.

Reverently pulls down the panties.

Spanks my bare ass and thighs.

Every time he removes a layer, he pulls back slightly on the intensity to build me up again.

Something happens to me when he begins to spank harder. Somehow the spanking goes deeper than the physical sadomasochism or the psychodrama of the role-play. The punishment becomes something I can use however I want. It is the confirmation of a resolution. I have never been religious but in a way spanking has become a ritualized absolution, except instead of sin it wipes away neurosis.

Nigel shoves me off of his lap and I stumble to my feet, rubbing my bottom. It has begun to redden from the blood being drawn to the surface.

"Now that you're warmed up, it's time for your caning."

I whimper but follow orders. I'm feeling euphoric, the endorphins rushing. I'm well into the place where submission feels like liberation and pain feels like passionate tenderness.

Nigel instructs me to pile all the pillows in the middle of the bed and lay across them with my ass raised in the air. Lying on the pillows relaxes me, and also absorbs the force of the impact so the body doesn't have to.

Tap-tap-tap-tap-*Thwack!*

The noise that a cane stroke elicits from my body is a rich, low moan.

Tap-tap-*THWACK!*

I can hear Nigel stalking slowly around me, taking in the sight of me admiring me. I know that his head is swimming, and he is concentrating very hard on remaining grounded.

THWACK!

When a cane lands across the skin with enough force, it bursts capillaries. A white welt rises at the spot where rattan meets skin. Sometimes the welts last for days and days. Sometimes purple and red bruises blossom out and the cane mark itself is a line of red surrounded by white. I love to watch bruises fade days after I am no longer close to the person who administered them. My ass will be tough like leather and stiff with arousal for many hours.

When Nigel is caning to mark, he always lays stripes parallel along the ass and down the thighs.

THWACK!

Afterwards, he holds me as he always does, bringing us both down from the realm of fantasy and endorphins. He rubs lotion onto my smarting skin. This aftercare is so important, like a cool-down lap after a race. If you don't do it, you could be sore the next day, or crash as a result of the disorientation that comes from not being well integrated back into "the real world."

We pull ourselves together and walk out of the dungeon side by side. He takes me out to dinner. We find a diner and order, as we always do after sessions, large quantities of red meat and potatoes and steamed vegetables and light beer and water, as if we had just returned home from a long journey.

Quinn Cassidy

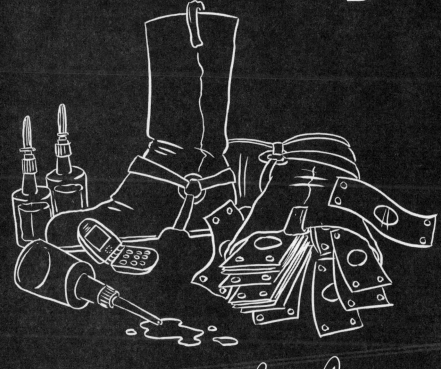

friendship

Quinn Cassidy

Here's the thing about being a sex worker in a world that hates and fears sex workers —you don't really want to tell people when you had a bad day on the job.

It's April 2012 and I'm flying from New York City to Detroit, Michigan, for an overnight session with a switch client I have never

met before, a man with a famous name. Another sex worker whom I trust has recommended him. She admits that he is "a little weird," but at this point I feel pretty skilled at handling "weird" and know it will be a very lucrative twenty-four hours.

I take a cab to LaGuardia for a 7am flight. A town car picks me up at the Detroit airport, taking me to my hotel room. I spend the afternoon with my client, who turns out to be manipulative, condescending, and cruel. He drinks two bottles of wine before 2pm, eventually switching to vodka. I can definitely handle a drink or two on the job, but he keeps insisting that I have more despite my firm protestations. He asks me about female friends who might one day join us for a double, ordering me to call them on my phone. He continues to insist that I try them again when they don't pick up, which I refuse to do. When I tell him one of my dominatrix friends is Latina, he dismisses the idea of sessioning with her, saying, "You know how it is, girls who aren't white just don't do it for me."

After several hours of this, he instructs me to change into lingerie in front of him. I have packed red and black Cuban heel stockings, shiny black pumps, and a dark purple chemise with ruffly pink garters. This is what I am wearing when we go into the bedroom, where he beats my ass for twenty minutes with a belt and a cane.

Corporal punishment is one of my favorite kinks. I have bottomed to this kind of play countless times in my life and I will continue to do so. It makes me cum, it makes me high on oxytocin; it can be therapeutic and cathartic and intimate. It's one of my favorite services to provide in session, and although I have had clients with a variety of skill levels, I am usually in control of my own limits and the negotiated power exchange.

What this client does to me is not BDSM. His aim is sloppy, and has no finesse, no timing, no dynamics. He just beats me, ruthlessly, and when I try to use all of my professional submissive tricks to persuade him to give me what I need, he ignores me.

What he does not understand about sadomasochism is that a kinky sadist does not *take* something from a masochist: the sadist seduces the masochist into surrendering. My client has intimidated me into a position where I am suffering through a severe caning; not as a consensual power exchange, but because I am terrified of what else he might do. I want to get through it so I can get the money he has promised me. The prospect of not being paid to do my job is worse than anything he is putting me through, or so I tell myself. I have developed the skills to cope with this, to rewrite the story of my strength in real time, a means to an end. I steel myself and breathe deeply and transform the pain into something I can use. I tell myself that I am tough, that I am a solider of love, and so I endure the fact that this man did not respect me.

This story is an anomaly, not a microcosm. Sex work doesn't have to be like this. BDSM doesn't have to be like this. I will not be broken by what is happening to me in this condo in Detroit. This man has the opportunity to experience everything I'm certain that he wants: the rush of power, the arousal of control, and the thrill of intimacy with a sexy dish in a purple chemise. He is squandering it, because he cannot help but take power too literally.

When he's done, I turn on a dime from the quivering girl with her bare ass in the air to the stern professional walking confidently down the hall in order to examine my ass in the mirror.

"You won't be bruised," he yells after me, sounding panicked.

Far, far worse than the fact that he has taken advantage of me, is the fact that he is insulting my intelligence.

I fucking know what a caning that is going to bruise feels like.

As he drives me back to my hotel, I distract him by talking endlessly about how much I love Bob Seger, the Stooges, Motown, and any other fucking Michigan band I can think of. When I am alone, I order an extra-large pizza with sausage and bell peppers and mushrooms and garlic. I charge it to the room. I sit in a very hot bath for a very long time, reading a book about Patti Smith's *Horses*, and then sleep the deep hotel sleep of a whore who doesn't have to worry about rent for a while. Around six in the morning, another town car takes me to the airport, another plane to Laguardia, and another cab to my Bed Stuy apartment, where Quinn Cassidy is asleep in my bed.

As I peel off my knee-length maroon leather jacket and polka-dot dress, Quinn stirs. We've barely seen each other since he arrived here from Oakland two days ago.

"Come live with me and we'll hustle New York for the summer," I had urged him on Skype, a few months earlier. "The beautiful boys will want to fuck you and the rich men will want to pay you."

"Mmm, c'mere baby...." Quinn murmurs, throwing back the comforter. When I wrench off a brown Frye boot, the wad of twenty-dollar bills I have stored there spills to the floor. Quinn manages a sleepy version of his cackling laugh. Androgyny flickers across his face like light from a passing train.

"Whore slapstick!" I announce, turning the other boot upside down and giving it a good shake for effect.

I am so exhausted that I don't even bother to collect my money before crawling naked between my lavender sheets and into Quinn's open arms.

When you live outside the law, you have to know who your real friends are.

"How was it, ho?" he asks, nuzzling his face into my neck. Quinn's voice shifts to a high register when he's bubbly, when he's chiding someone, when he's surprised. Enraptured by his enthusiastic charms, you might never imagine that he's also capable of an intimidating, guttural growl.

"It was the opposite in every way of most sessions I've had in my life," I sigh.

In the arms of another whore, suddenly everything is fine. It's over. I lived, and my bruises will heal. My money is strewn across my own floor and I will never see that client again.

We giggle over the absurdities that make our work worthwhile. The little victories like hitting the down button on the elevator with the kick of a high heel. All the while he nods, knowingly, encouragingly, holds me tighter, and calms me.

I marvel that a body so lean could be so comfortable and that someone almost a decade younger could make me feel so mothered and safe.

"I don't want to tell anyone this story," I say to him. "I want to tell them about Jean the Spy, who comes to session with elaborate scripts of espionage. I want to tell them about the men who pay just to reverently jiggle my ass for two hours, or watch me cum, or call me a beautiful goddess. I want to tell them about the retired punk rocker client who booked me a night in the Bowery Hotel, left after a lovely three hour tease and denial session, and how you brought a bunch of faggots over and we drank beers in the enormous bath and had a bunch of gay sex and smoked cigars and Dane almost fell off the roof."

"Those stories belong to us," Quinn reminds me. "We need to be able to tell the dark stories, so that people know the difference."

Quinn plays with my nipples while we talk,

pressing them down with the pads of his fingers and watching them bounce slowly back into shape. He does this with the absentmindedness of someone playing with his own body.

Here's the thing about being a sex worker—other sex workers are the reason you survive.

"Let me make you breakfast," says Quinn.

❧

Quinn is tired of being told he looks like Mick Jagger.

Still, the comparison—the juicy lips, the sensuality that is both tender and menacing, the audacity of such a lithe body taking up so much space—bears repeating. Sorry, Quinn.

I'm reminded of Lester Bang's description of Jagger: "a spastic flap-lipped tornado writhing from here to a million steaming snatches and beyond in one undifferentiated erogenous mass, a mess and a spectacle all at the same time."

Replace the "steaming snatches" with "a million itchy assholes" and you might begin to have an idea of why, on the basis of sex appeal alone, Quinn is such a successful rent boy.

If you run into Quinn wearing full face, he is likely to be dripping with cat-eye liquid liner. Lips so vampish it's as if they had finally swollen until the blood was ready to burst through their thin membranes. Chestnut hair gathered on his head. A thrift store dress, synthetic fabric hanging just right because Quinn, like many femme men, has a better body for women's evening wear than most females do.

But it takes more than sex appeal to make a good whore—or, at least, a whore with the kind of staying power Quinn possesses. Quinn is a savvy hustler. He knows how to make you feel real, real special. He also knows how to take care of himself.

Now, with the bobby pins out, Quinn has the quality of an eccentric showbiz queen in her dressing room between acts. He has a smoker's tough lined face, though he has been trying for months with some success to quit. Everything he does, he does with a flourish.

As Quinn fries up bacon, thin-sliced potatoes, white cheddar, and collard greens in the cast iron skillet, I gather all of our silicon dicks and plugs—soiled for reasons both personal and professional—and throw them in a deep pot to disinfect them.

In the view from my tall kitchen window, all of Brooklyn seems to be happening in one Bed Stuy intersection. You can get your checks cashed and you can do your laundry and you can buy tall-cans and fried chicken and pizza with lasagna on top. During the year's first heat wave, the concrete sea lion in the playground across the street began spouting water as if in competition with all the sprung fire hydrants. It has been a fountain ever since, cooling the otherwise stifling air. The alto sax guy is sitting in front of the bodega again, accompanying "Love on Top" and

"Juicy" and "Try A Little Tenderness" as those songs pass by, carried on southbound sound systems.

I take the kettle off the stove for coffee and Quinn's cell phone buzzes. When he answers, his lips stretch from ear to ear. It's not that he's happy so much as he's putting a smile on his voice. I understand what is happening because I perform that same click when my clients call me: a subtle transformation, an instant preview. We both know how to a refocus into a cheery upward lilt, as if we haven't a care in all the world.

It's something you can spot in when you've been doing this for a while.

My erotic area of expertise is the *mind*-fuck. Unlike a dancer, who puts on a show just out of arm's reach, I play the role of a woman who physically and psychologically rubs your face in the fact that you can't have what you want. Force, control, restraint, torture, agony, temptation: these are the tools of my trade. When I started performing in and producing porn, I made it my business to give anyone with a few bucks to burn a glimpse into a sexual underground of queers, exhibitionists, and kinky perverts. I am, in a word, a tease.

Quinn, on the other hand, is a provider of satisfaction. He is twenty-two and has been an escort his entire adult life. Sure, there's flirtation and talent to his job. But he's a Rent Boy—you borrow his body and his charms by the hour, and then return it to be loaned out another day.

I met Quinn in the spring of 2011 through fellow

queer pornographer James Darling. In fact, the first time I ever laid eyes on Quinn was on James' video blog. In the video, James is walking down Mission Street, his shaky Flipcam following a tough-looking guy about his age. The guy wears 2 gauge bone earrings and a leather motorcycle jacket with a white skeleton stencil spray-painted on the back.

"Can you tell us your name?" asks the disembodied voice of James Darling, sounding very much like he is cruising the subject of his video.

"I'm Quinn Valentine," the subject smirks, staring off and away from the camera.

The couple had just shot a Valentine's Day scene for *Heavenly Spire,* a side project of *Crash Pad Series* director Shine Louise Houston and videographer Tristan Crane. Most of the clips on this site are of men discussing their sexuality, masturbating for the camera, and occasionally having sex with one another. It's rare to find videos of trans men and cis men together, especially in a scene as romantic as the one that James and Quinn shot that day.

In James' Behind the Scenes Flipcam clip, Quinn is impassioned and insistent, speaking in assertive extremes like, "It was *fantastic,* " and, "If you get a chance to make porn with a partner, do it, it's *magical.*"

He strides quickly along the sidewalk; James seems to be struggling to both hold the camera and keep up.

Quinn's rough beauty made an impression on me, but so did the way he describes being a gay male who loves trans men: "I love having my chin drenched after I blow somebody."

James also told me that his new boyfriend took it in the ass like a champ. So when I was shooting an educational movie about strap-on sex for Smitten Kitten, and looking to cast a male bottom, I looked up Quinn Valentine. (He would later change his stage surname to Cassidy.)

He was a dream to work with: sweet, polite, and punctual. For his interview, he described himself as a "queer femme cis-male poly switch" who worshipped Pat Benatar. Quinn's scene partner was Sophia St James, a voluptuous queer femme performer who fucked him with an enormous strap-on dildo for hours. Not only did Quinn make good on his reputation, but he also behaved as if he was utterly in love with Sophia.

At the end of the shoot, he revealed that he had only had sex with a woman once before. We were all totally shocked.

This isn't to say Quinn's affection was phony. This is not a case of someone who knows how to turn phoniness on and off. Rather, Quinn is capable of seeing the lovability of anyone in any situation. He is capable of accessing a genuine connection and sharing it.

Quinn is well aware of this skill. It's the same reason he was good at retail. He gets off on bringing other people pleasure.

You want to hire Quinn because of his Satanic good looks, and almost certainly because of his unique combination of feminine grace and macho libido. You hire him for those damn lips, for those wild eyes, for his lean physique. You hire him because he can get it up and keep it up, and because he has a big beautiful cock. You hire him because he does, as promised, take it like a champ, and is always careful to be clean (Quinn refers to giving himself an enema as "brushing my teeth"). You hire him because he gives a mean blowjob. You hire him because he is young but very sexually evolved. But mostly, I think you hire him for this reason:

As Quinn finishes his phone conversation with that evening's client, he catches me studying him. We lock eyes and he lays it on just a little thicker for my benefit as he tells his client he "just can't *wait*" to see him later. Snapping his cell shut, he bows.

"I am very good at telling lies that are the truth," he says.

*

That afternoon Quinn and I head to Prospect Park to take a stroll through our minds. We have two little heart-shaped chocolates blended with psilocybin mushrooms. Our ads have been up this month and we are in demand. The city's summer pores are wide open and everyone wants whatever it is, exactly, that we're selling.

Today we are not for sale.

Quinn doses himself right after our long breakfast. I want for us to be in step, so I unwrap the chocolate from its pink tin foil and say, "Here goes nuthin'."

As we wait for the Southbound B15 I start to feel over-stimulated and panicky.

"Don't worry," Quinn says, staring off into the distance not only of space but of time as well. "You're safe with me."

And because he says it, it is so.

The bus arrives and I remember how the Metrocard is eaten and spat out again, how to brightly say *Thank You,* how to feel out my equilibrium when the ground becomes unstable.

Quinn nestles me into a seat by the window. I manage to wedge both my head and right headphone onto his shoulder.

I doze, and a red velvet curtain is pulled aside. I am onstage, a towering spectacular sparkling creature bolstered by a shuddering base, four to the floor. I am surrounded by revelers, all of them men, all of them worshipping me. Some bring me gold coins. Some dance, some tell me stories, some fawn over me. Some prostrate themselves before me, asses in the air.

"I will empty myself completely for you," says one.

"I've got exactly what you need," says another.

"We will make you our New Queen Of The Endless Night!" they cry in unison.

This filthy, base story is still going on in New

York City, after hours, behind closed doors. A hustle here, and a hustle there.

I feel swollen with power, but I am old enough to recognize when someone is going for my jugular: the pumping coursing lifeblood that is my Pride.

"No, New York!" I intone to the boys. "I will *show* you what kind of Queen I am! I will only collect the spoils that I have earned."

Having made my declaration, I look around for a way out, for a glorious dramatic exit. Right on cue, Quinn is standing at the base of the stage. He gazes up at me, extending a gentlemanly palm. I grab it and leap lightly off the pedestal.

Sure enough, no one notices my smooth escape. The men continue to dance without missing a beat. Almost certainly, they raise another avatar to the stage to replace me, and maybe she is the right one for all that manic control. I don't know, though, because I don't look back as we move, hands clutched, easy like liquid, through the crowd, towards the door, searching for a quiet place outdoors to get sunburned and work on some sentences.

I blink my eyes open and feel Quinn's arm around me. Sitting up slowly, I push my headphones back.

"You were dancing ever so slightly," he tells me.

I open my mouth to explain, and can only giggle. Quinn is intoxicated with my glee and soon we are tittering, our hands over one another's mouths.

"Oh!" I say suddenly, noticing we're approaching Eastern Parkway.

"This is us!"

On that beat, the bus lurches to a stop. Of one mind, we spring into action, grabbing our bags, dashing for the door, hitting the street again.

Acknowledgments
December 2014

Sex work is the cultural framework through which I view the subjects of this book, but it is not the subject of the book itself. A book about sex work would be incomplete without more diversity. I hope to devote my future work to that.

Thank you from the bottom of my slutty heart to the subjects of this book, James Darling, Bianca Stone, Sage Travigne, Quinn Cassidy, and Nigel Matthews, who trusted me with their stories—both the glamorous and shadow sides. The original reporting for this project was finished in 2013, but all of their stories continue.

This book is for sex workers everywhere, and especially those who have meant the world to me, who have taught workshops and done doubles with me and survived with me: Casey Grey, Rosa Fletcher, Andre Shakti, Mickey Mod, Arabelle Raphael, Maggie Mayhem, Lorelei Lee, Siouxsie Q, Nikki Silver, everyone I worked with at the Gates, and everyone who has shared their resources with me. Also, thank you for having sex with me for money: that was awesome.

Special thank you to Alice Truax, who was my thesis advisor, and gave me the best micro-edits and counseling I could hope to have. Thanks also to Verlyn Klinkenborg, for teaching me about sentences and taking extra care with this material. Thanks to Raygun Louise and Natasha Lewis for astral fitness, and to everyone who workshopped my thesis. Thanks to my writing teachers, Jo Ann Beard, Suzanne Gardinier, Vijay Seshadri, Dan Fishback, and Randall Kenan; and to all my Lambda retreat nonfiction possums, especially Joe Osmundson for his close reading of a final draft (with both Gay Talese and Eileen Myles sitting nearby, against all probability!). Thanks to Johnny Blazes for reminding me that a book about sex can give you a boner.

Thank you to my heroes who gave this book early reviews and endorsements. Special thanks to Carol Queen for also writing my letter of recommendation to graduate school.

Thank you to Gregory Kaplan for being a dreamer.

Thank you to Sarah Patterson and Zil Goldstein of the Persist Health Project, Audacia Ray of the Red Umbrella Project, as well as St James, SWOP, and HIPS, and everyone who is working so hard for the rights of sex workers.

To the people who have given me professional opportunities and artistic community—Shine Louise Houston, Maxwell Lander, S. Bear Bergman, Sinclair Sexsmith, Reid Mihalko, Madison Young, everyone at Pink and White Productions, everyone at Good For Her and the Feminist Porn Awards, and Jennifer Pritchett and the folks at Smitten Kitten.

I owe my life to my friends and family who never

judged me: Andrea, Lisa, Ryan, Ariel, Mark, Lauren, Beth, Dusty, Cailin, Amanda, my mom, my dad, and my sister.

I have the sweetest bear who is mine all mine, who wants me to have all the adventures and says, "Tell me stories." Here are some, and you'll be the first to hear every one from now on. Thanks for the leather and the gold.